THE

COUNTRY DANCE BOOK

PART IV.

CONTAINING

FORTY-THREE COUNTRY DANCES

FROM

THE ENGLISH DANCING MASTER

(1650—1728)

DESCRIBED BY

CECIL J. SHARP

AND

GEORGE BUTTERWORTH.

British Library Cataloguing-in-Publication Data
A catalogue record for this book is available from
the British Library

Folk Music

Folk music includes both traditional music and the genre that evolved from it during the twentieth century folk revival. Traditional folk music has been broadly defined as music transmitted orally, without a single 'composer', as contrasted with commercial and classical styles.

A consistent and all-encompassing definition of traditional folk music is elusive however. The terms *folk music*, *folk song*, and *folk dance* are comparatively recent expressions. They are extensions of the term *folklore*, which was coined in 1846 by the English antiquarian William Thoms to describe 'the traditions, customs, and superstitions of the uncultured classes.' The term is further derived from the German expression *Volk*, in the sense of 'the people as a whole' as applied to popular and national music by Johann Gottfried Herder and the German Romantics over half a century earlier. The emergence of the term 'folk' coincided with the mid-nineteenth century outburst of national feeling all over Europe, particularly at the edges of Europe, where national identity was most strongly asserted.

Folk music may tend to have certain characteristics but it cannot clearly be differentiated in purely musical terms. One meaning often given is that of 'old songs, with no known composers', another is that of music that has been submitted to an evolutionary 'process of oral transmission.... the fashioning and re-fashioning of the music by the community that give it its folk character.' For scholars such as Béla Bartók, (a Hungarian composer and pianist who collected and studied folk music – as one of the founders of comparative musicology and ethnomusicology) there was a sense of the music of the country as distinct from that of the town. Folk music was seen as the authentic expression of a way of life now past or about to disappear, particularly in a community uninfluenced by modern 'artistic' and commercial music.

Throughout most of human prehistory and history, listening to recorded music was not possible. Music was made by common people during both their work and leisure. The work of economic production was often manual and communal. Manual labour often included singing by the workers, which served several practical purposes. It reduced the boredom of repetitive tasks, it kept the rhythm during synchronized pushes and pulls, and it set the pace of many activities such as planting, weeding, reaping, threshing, weaving, and milling. In leisure time, singing and playing musical instruments were common forms of entertainment and history-telling – even more common than today, when electrically enabled technologies made these forms of information-sharing competitive.

Opinions differ greatly on the origins of folk music. Some said it was art music that was changed and probably debased by oral transmission – others said it reflects the character of the race that produced it. 'Individual' and 'Collective' theories of its dissemination abound. Traditionally, the cultural transmission of folk music is through learning by ear, although notation may also be used, and traditional cultures that did not rely on written music produced work that was exceedingly difficult to categorise.

Despite this, many scholars attempted just such an endeavour, and the English term 'folklore', entered the vocabulary of many continental European nations, each of which had its folk-song collectors and revivalists.

Cecil Sharp (the founding father of the folklore revival in England in the early twentieth century) had an influential idea about the process of folk variation: he felt that the competing variants of a traditional song would undergo a process akin to biological natural selection: only those new variants that were the most appealing to ordinary singers would be picked up by others and transmitted onward in time. Thus, over time we would expect each traditional song to become aesthetically ever more appealing — it would be collectively composed to perfection, as it were, by the community.

The distinction between 'authentic' folk and national and popular song in general has always been loose. The International Folk Music Council definition allows that the term can also apply to music that 'has originated with an individual composer and has subsequently been absorbed into the unwritten, living tradition of a community.' But the term does not cover a song, dance, or tune that has been taken over ready-made and remains unchanged. Apart from instrumental music that forms a part of traditional folk music, especially dance music traditions, much traditional folk music is vocal music, since the instrument that makes such music is usually handy. As such, most traditional folk music has meaningful, historically significant lyrics.

Narrative verse looms large in the traditional folk music of many cultures. This encompasses such forms as traditional epic poetry, much of which was meant originally for oral performance, sometimes accompanied by instruments. Many epic poems of various cultures were pieced together from shorter pieces of traditional narrative verse, which explains their episodic structure and often their *in medias res* plot developments. Other forms of traditional narrative verse (and hence folkloric singing) relate the outcomes of battles and other tragedies or natural disasters. Sometimes, as in the triumphant *Song of Deborah* found in the Biblical *Book of Judges*, these songs celebrate victory. Laments for lost battles and wars, and the lives lost in them, are equally prominent in many traditions; these laments keeping alive the cause for which the battle was fought.

Hymns and other forms of religious music are often of traditional and unknown origin, though their inclusion in the folkloric canon is debatable. Western musical notation was originally created to preserve the lines of Gregorian chant, which before its invention was taught as an oral tradition in monastic communities. Traditional songs such as *Green grow the rushes* (originating in the nineteenth century) present religious lore in a mnemonic form. In the Western world, Christmas carols and other traditional songs also preserve religious lore in song form. Other common forms of folk signing include work songs with 'call and response' structures, designed to coordinate labourer's efforts. Often arising in the terrible times of slavery and forced labour, they were frequently, but not invariably composed by the community that sung them. In the American armed forces, a lively tradition of jody calls

('Duckworth chants') are sung while soldiers are on the march, and all over the world, professional sailors make great use of sea shanties. Nursery rhymes, love poetry and nonsense verse also are also frequent subjects of traditional folk songs.

Music transmitted by word of mouth through a community, in time, develops many variants. This kind of transmission cannot produce word-for-word and note-for-note accuracy, which contrariwise – has proved to be the genre's greatest weakness, though also, its ultimate strength. Indeed, many traditional singers quite creatively and deliberately modify the material they learn. Because variants proliferate naturally, it is naive to believe that there is such a thing as the single 'authentic' version of a folksong. Despite this, by keeping such music actively alive, developing lyrics and tunes, and keeping it relevant within a community, the great tradition of folk singing has been kept alive. It is hoped the current reader enjoys this book on the subject, and is encouraged to find out more.

This Book is issued in connection with " Country Dance Tunes "

(Sets VII. and VIII., price 1s. 6d. each.)

LONDON: NOVELLO AND COMPANY, LTD.

CONTENTS.

LONGWAYS FOR AS MANY AS WILL.

THE DANCE.

THE ROOM.

THE following diagram is a ground plan of the room in which the dances are supposed to take place :—

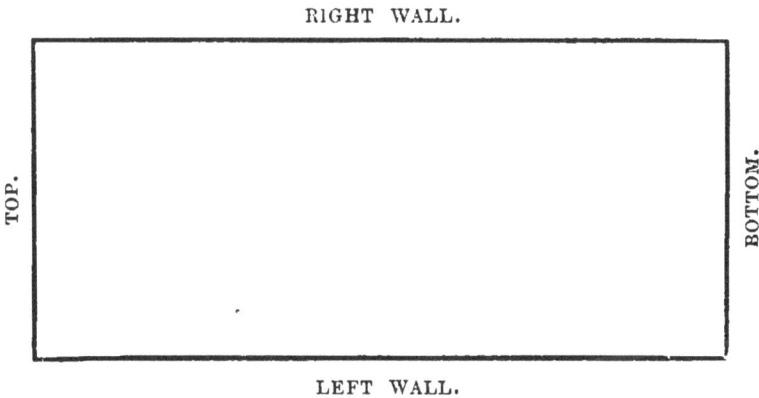

RIGHT WALL.

TOP.

BOTTOM.

LEFT WALL.

A diagram, showing the initial disposition of the dancers, is printed at the head of the notation of each dance, and placed so that its four sides correspond with the four sides of the room as depicted in the above plan. That is, the upper and lower sides of the diagram represent, respectively, the right and left walls of the room ; its left and right sides the top and bottom.

In Playford's time, the top of the room was called *the Presence*, alluding to the dais upon which the spectators were seated. The expression *facing the Presence* means, therefore, facing up, *i.e.*, toward the top of the room ; while *back to the Presence* means facing down, toward the bottom of the room.

TECHNICAL TERMS AND SYMBOLS.

In the following pages, certain symbols and technical expressions are used. These will now be defined.

O = man ; ☐ = woman.

r. = a step taken with the right foot ; l. = a step taken with the left foot.

h.r. = a hop off the right foot ; l.r. = a hop off the left foot.

f.t. = feet-together.

∩   a spring.

A *Longways dance* is one in which the performers take partners and stand in two parallel lines, those on the *men's side* facing the right wall, those on the *women's side* facing the left wall.

The *General Set* denotes the above formation, *i.e.*, the area enclosed by the dancers.

A *Progressive movement*, or *figure*, is one which leaves the dancers relatively in different positions.

A *Progressive dance* consists of the repetition, for an indefinite number of times, of a series of movements one of which is progressive, the execution of each repetition resulting, therefore, in a change of position of some, or all of the performers. Each performance of one complete series of movements is called a *Round*.

There are two types of progression called, respectively, *Whole-set* and *Minor-set*.

In a *Whole-set* dance the progression is effected by the transference of the top couple to the bottom of the General Set, each of the remaining couples moving up one place. The *Minor-set* dance is one in which the figures contained in each round are performed simultaneously by subsidiary groups of two (*duple*), or three (*triple*), adjacent couples.

A *neutral* dancer is one who is passive during the performance of a round. Normally, in a Minor-set dance, each couple, on reaching either end of the General Set, remains neutral during the next round, and sometimes the following one as well.*

The disposition of the dancers in a longways dance is said to be *proper* when men and women are on their own sides; and *improper* when the men are on the women's side and the women on the men's.

In dances, or figures, in which two couples only are engaged, the terms *contrary woman* and *contrary man* are used to denote the woman or man other than the partner.

When two dancers, standing side by side, are directed to *take hands* they are to join inside hands : that is, the right hand of one with the left hand of the other, if the two face the same way ; and right hands or left hands, if they face in opposite directions. When they are directed to take, or give, right or left hands, they are to join right with right, or left with left.

To *cross hands* the man takes the right and left hands of the woman with, respectively, his right and left hands, the right hands being held above the left.

When two dancers face one another and are directed to take *both hands,* they are to join right with left and left with right.

To pass *by the right* is to pass right shoulder to right shoulder ; *by the left,* left shoulder to left shoulder.

When two dancers pass each other they should always, unless otherwise directed, pass each other by the right.

When a woman's path crosses that of a man's, the man should allow the woman to pass first and in front of him.

---

* For further and more detailed information on this point see *The Country Dance Book,* Part I., pp. 13—24.

When one dancer is told to *lead* another, the two join right or left hands according as the second dancer stands on the right or left hand of the leader.

To *cast off* is to turn outward and dance outside the General Set.

To *cast up* or *cast down* is to turn outward and move up or down outside the General Set.

To *fall* hither or thither is to dance backwards; to *lead*, or *move*, is to dance forwards.

To make a *half-turn* is to turn through half a circle and face in the opposite direction; to make a *whole-turn* is to make a complete revolution.

The terms *clockwise* and *counter-clockwise* are self-explanatory and refer to the direction of circular movements.

THE MUSIC.

The several strains of each dance-air will be marked in the music book and in the notation by means of capital letters, A, B, C, etc. When a strain is played more than once in a Part it will be marked A1, B1, C1, etc., on its first performance, and A2, B2, C2, A3, B3, etc., in subsequent repetitions.

It will be found that most of the dances in this collection are divided into two or more Parts. John Essex quaintly but aptly likened these divisions to " the several verses of songs upon the same tune ".

In non-progressive dances, the division is made merely for the sake of clearness in description; the Parts are intended to follow on without pause.

When, however, a progressive movement occurs in one or other of the figures of a Part, that Part must be repeated as often as the dancers decree. The usual practice is to repeat the Part until the leader has returned to his original place at the top of the General Set.

Progressive figures will be marked as such in the notation ; while the Parts in which they occur will be headed " Whole-Set", " Duple Minor-Set", etc., according to the nature of the progression.

THE STEPS.

Country Dance steps always fall on the main beats of the bar, whether the time be simple or compound. When the step itself is a compound one, that is, when it consists of more than one movement, the accented movement always falls upon the beginning of the beat.

RUNNING-STEP.

A bounding or slow running step, executed upon the ball of the foot with a moderate amount of spring, forward rather than upward, and with limbs relaxed. The arms, held loosely, should be slightly bent at the elbow and allowed to swing naturally and rhythmically.

In the notation this step will be called :—

r.s. (running-step).

WALKING-STEP.

This is a springy walking step executed, at any rate by the men, with a nonchalant bearing and a certain jauntiness of manner not easily described. Technically, the fundamental distinction between the ordinary walking-step and that used in the country dance is that in the former the weight of the body is gradually transferred from one foot to the other (both feet, at one moment of the movement, being on the ground at the same time), and each step is taken first on the heel and then on the ball of the foot ; whereas, in the country-dance walking-step, the movement from one foot to the other is effected by means of a very small spring and is executed entirely on the ball of the foot. In other words, the step is in reality a modified form of the running-step, in which the spring, though present, is scarcely noticeable.

In the notation this will be called :—

w.s. (walking-step).

SKIPPING-STEP.

This is a step and hop first on one foot and then on the other. The hop is made forward rather than up, and should raise the body as little as possible. When the steps are long and the motion rapid, the hop should be scarcely perceptible.

The accent is on the step, which must fall, therefore, on the beginning of the beat. The hop falls on the last quarter, or the last third of the beat, according as the latter is simple or compound, thus :—

$\frac{2}{2}$ l. h.l. r. b.r. | l. h.l. r. b.r. |

OR

$\frac{6}{8}$ r. h.r. l. h.l. | r. h.r. l. h.l. |

In the notation this step will be called :—

sk.s. (skipping-step).

THE SLIP.

This, like the preceding, is a compound step. It is used in moving sideways along the straight, or around a circle, the dancer facing at right angles to the line of motion.

The performer stands with feet apart. If moving, say, to the left, a low spring is made off the left foot and the weight of the body transferred to the right foot, which alights close to the spot just vacated by the left foot. The left foot then falls to the ground, twelve inches or more to the side, a spring is again made off it, with a side thrust imparted by the right foot,' and the movements are repeated. The legs are thus alternately opening and closing, scissors-fashion.

The accent falls on the foot off which the spring is made, that is, the left or right, according as the motion is toward the left or right, thus : —

Moving to the left.

l.　r.　l.　r.　l.　r.　l.　r.

Moving to the right.

r.　l.　r.　l.　r.　l.　r.　l.

The slip is used, though not invariably, in ring movements and whenever the dancers are directed to move sideways, or " slip " to right or left.

THE DOUBLE-HOP.

This is sometimes used in ring movements, as an alternative to the preceding step. It is a variant of the Slip, in which the feet, instead of taking the ground one after the other, alight together, about six inches apart. The movement is, therefore, a series of jumps or double-hops.

THE SINGLE.

This consists of two movements. A step forward, or to the side, is made with one foot, say, the right, and the weight of the body supported upon it. The left foot is then drawn up and the heel placed in the hollow of the right foot (one bar).

As the left foot is moved up to the right, the body is raised upon the instep of the right foot, and lowered as the feet come together.   These movements are shown in the following diagram :—

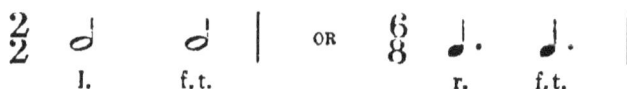

THE DOUBLE.

The double is three steps, forward or backward, followed by " feet-together," thus :—

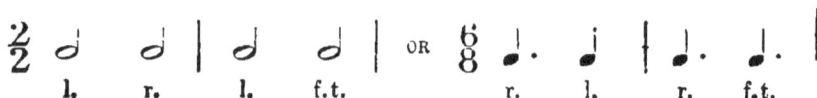

THE FIGURES.

FIGURE 1.

TURN SINGLE.

The dancer moves round in a small circle, clockwise (unless otherwise directed), taking four small running-steps,* beginning with the right foot.   When the turn is directed to be made counter-clockwise, the first step is taken with the left foot.

Care must be taken to keep the body erect, but not stiff, and to time the turn so that the dancer reaches his original position exactly on the conclusion of the last step.

FIGURE 2.

THE SET.

This is a formal movement of courtesy, addressed by one dancer to another or, more frequently, by two dancers to each

---

* In dances in triple time the movement is completed in three steps.

other, simultaneously. It consists of a single to the right, followed by a single to the left (two bars), thus :—

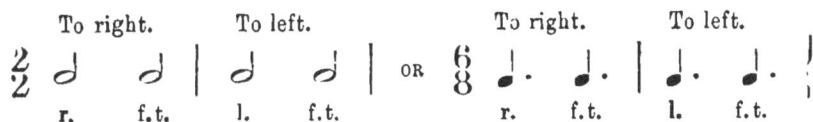

FIGURE 3.

THE SET-AND-HONOUR.

In certain dances four instead of two bars are allotted to the Set. This may be simply an abbreviation, or misprint, for Set-and-turn-single ; or it may bear a literal interpretation, in which case it is, perhaps, advisable to interpolate the Honour (Fig. 11, p. 16) after each single, thus :—

Whenever set-and-honour occurs in the text, performers may either execute it in the way just described, or substitute the set-and-turn-single.

FIGURE 4.

THE SIDE.

This, like the set, is a movement of courtesy, performed by two dancers, usually partners, but not necessarily so.

The two dancers face each other and then move forward a double (w.s. or r.s.) obliquely to the right, passing by the left, and on the last step (f.t.) making a half-turn counter-clockwise and so facing each other (two bars). This completes the first half of the movement and is called *side to the right*. In the second half of the movement—*side to the left*—the dancers retrace their steps along the same tracks and return to their original places, beginning with the left foot, moving obliquely to the left, passing by the right, and turning clockwise on the "feet-together" to face each other, thus :—

To right..................Half-turn.   Back............to............Position.

r.   l.   r.   f.t.   l.   r.   l.   f.t.

OR

To right..................Half-turn.   Back............to............Position.

r.   l.   r.   f.t.   l.   r.   l.   f.t.

The dancers must remember to face each other at the beginning of each movement, to pass close to each other shoulder to shoulder, and always to face in the direction in which they are moving.

FIGURE 5.

ARM WITH THE RIGHT.

Two performers, usually partners, meet, link right arms, swing round a complete circle clockwise, separate and fall back to places (r.s.) (four bars). The precise moment at which the dancers unlink depends upon circumstances, but it is usually on the fifth or sixth step.

FIGURE 6.

ARM WITH THE LEFT.

This is similar to the preceding movement, the dancers linking left instead of right arms, and swinging round counter-clockwise instead of clockwise.

FIGURE 7.

ALL LEAD UP A DOUBLE AND FALL BACK A DOUBLE TO PLACES.

Couples stand in column formation, facing up. Each man then leads his partner up a double and, without turning or releasing hands, falls back a double (four bars).

FIGURE 8.

ALL LEAD UP A DOUBLE, CHANGE HANDS AND LEAD BACK

A DOUBLE.

All lead up a double as in the preceding figure. They then release and change hands, make a half-turn toward each other, face downwards, and lead a double back to places (four bars).

FIGURE 9.

HANDS-THREE, HANDS-FOUR, ETC.

Three or more dancers, as directed, extend and join hands, dance round in a ring clockwise, facing centre, make one complete circuit, separate, and return to places.

If more or less than one circuit is to be made, specific instructions to that effect will be given in the notation, *e.g.*, half-way round, once-and-a-half round, etc. In the absence of any such directions it is to be understood that one complete circuit is to be danced.

The performers should clasp hands firmly, lean outward, and not dance too daintily. When the movement is followed by a repetition in the reverse direction, the dancers, without releasing hands, may stamp on the first beat of the second movement.

Occasionally, this figure is performed facing outward, that is, with backs toward the centre. Whenever this occurs special instructions to that effect will be given in the notation.

FIGURE 10.

THE TURN.

Two dancers face each other, join both hands, swing round clockwise, separate, and return to places.

In swinging, performers should clasp hands firmly, and lean outward as in the ring movement. If either the skipping- or the running-step be used the feet should be slightly crossed so that the dancers may face each other throughout the movement.

FIGURE 11.

THE HONOUR.

This, like the Set, is a formal movement of courtesy addressed by one dancer to another, or by two dancers to each other simultaneously.

In making the honour, the woman curtseys, and the man bows and, if he is wearing one, raises his hat.

The old custom was for partners to honour each other at the beginning and at the close of each dance—the latter should never be omitted. The movement should always be done in rhythm with the music.

FIGURE 12.

HALF-POUSSETTE.

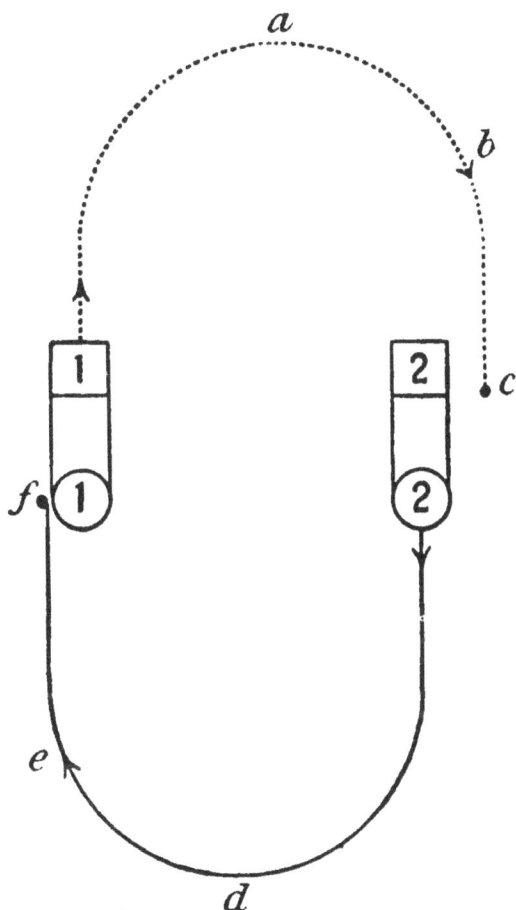

This is performed by two adjacent couples.

Each man faces his partner and takes her by both hands. The arms must be held out straight, and very nearly shoulder high.

First man, pushing his partner before him, moves four steps along dotted line to *a*, and then falls back four steps along the line *a b c* into the second couple's place, pulling his partner after him.

Simultaneously, second man, pulling his partner with him, falls back four steps along unbroken line to *d*, and then moves forward four steps along the line *d e f* into the first couple's place (four bars).

The above movement is called the half-poussette, and is, of course, a progressive figure.

When the half-poussette is followed by a repetition of the same movement, each couple describing a complete circle or ellipse, the figure is called the whole-poussette.

FIGURE 13.

BACK-TO-BACK.

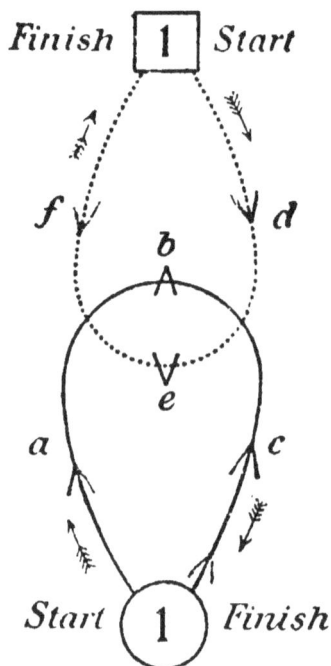

First man and first woman face each other and move forward, the man along the line *a b*, the woman along the dotted line *d e*. They pass by the right, move round each other, back to back, and fall back to places, the man along the line *b c*, the woman along the dotted line *e f*.

The arrow heads in the diagram show the positions of the dancers at the end of each bar and point in the directions in which they are facing. The arrows outside the lines show the direction in which the dancers move.

FIGURE 14.

WHOLE-GIP FACING CENTRE.

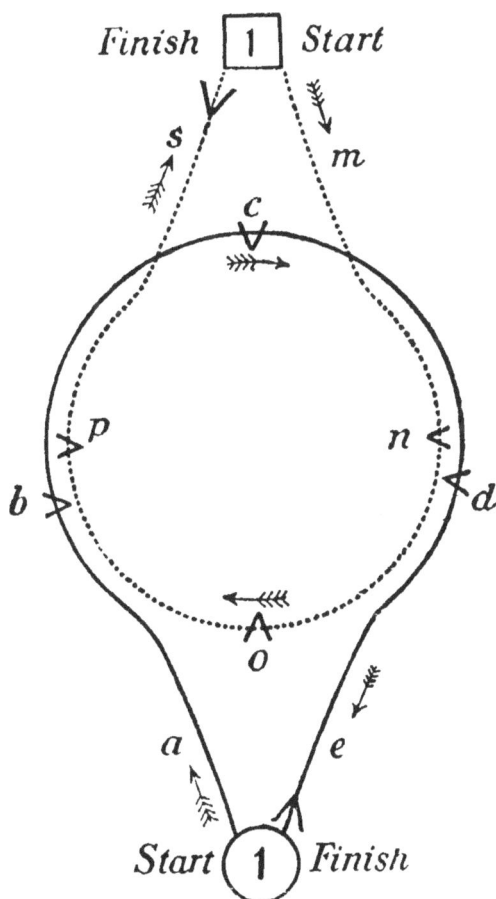

First man moves forward along line *a*, dances round circle *b c d*, keeping his face toward the centre, and falls back along line *d e* to place; while first woman dances along dotted line *m*, moves round circle *n o p*, keeping her face toward the centre, and falls back along dotted line *p s* to place (four bars).

The arrows and arrow heads have the same signification as in the preceding figure.

FIGURE 15.

WHOLE-GIP FACING OUTWARD.

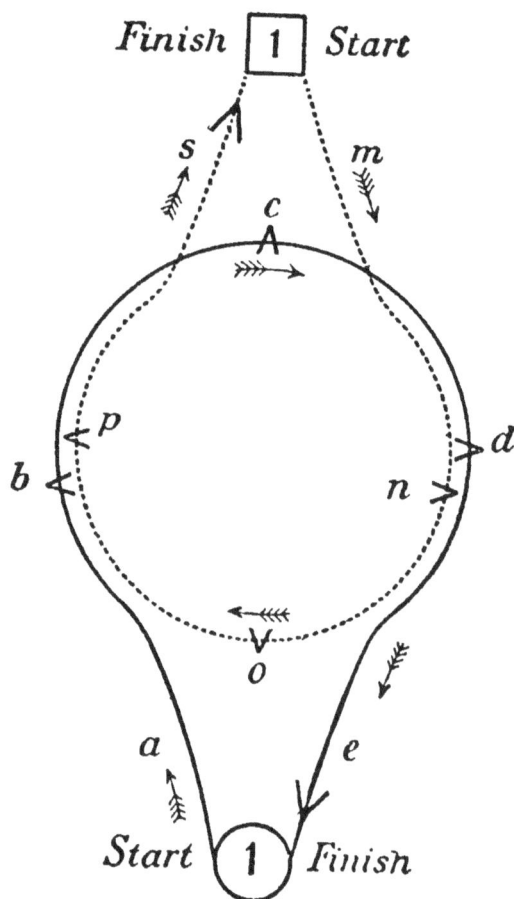

First man moves along line *a* and dances round circle *b c d*, facing outward, to place; while first woman moves along dotted line *m*, dances round circle *n o p*, facing outward, and moves along dotted line *p s* to place (four bars).

FIGURE 16.

RIGHT-HANDS-ACROSS.

This is performed usually by four dancers (say, first and second couples), but occasionally by three.

In the former case, first man and second woman join right hands, while second man and first woman do the same. Holding their hands close together, chin-high, the four dancers dance round clockwise to places, all facing in the direction in which they are moving.

When three performers only are dancing, two of them clasp right hands while the third places his right hand on the hands of the others.

FIGURE 17.

LEFT-HANDS-ACROSS.

This is very similar to the preceding figure, the dancers joining left instead of right hands and dancing round counterclockwise instead of clockwise.

It is to be understood that in both of these figures the dancers make one complete circuit unless specific instructions to the contrary are given.

THE HEY.

The Hey may be defined as the rhythmical interlacing in serpentine fashion of two groups of dancers, moving in single file and in opposite directions.

The figure assumes different forms according to the disposition of the dancers. These varieties, however, fall naturally into two main types according as the track described by the dancers—disregarding the deviations made by them in passing one another—is (1) a straight line, or (2) the perimeter of a closed figure, circle or ellipse.

The second of these species, as the simpler of the two, will be first explained.

FIGURE 18.

THE CIRCULAR HEY.

In the analysis that follows the circle will, for the sake of convenience, be used throughout to represent the track described by the dancers in this form of the figure. In the round dance the track will, of course, be a true circle ; while in the square dance it will become one as soon as the movement has begun. On the other hand, in a longways dance, the formation will be elliptical, rather than circular, but this will not affect the validity of the following explanation.

In the circular-hey the dancers, who must be even in number, are stationed, at equal distances, around the circumference of a circle, facing alternately in opposite directions, thus :—

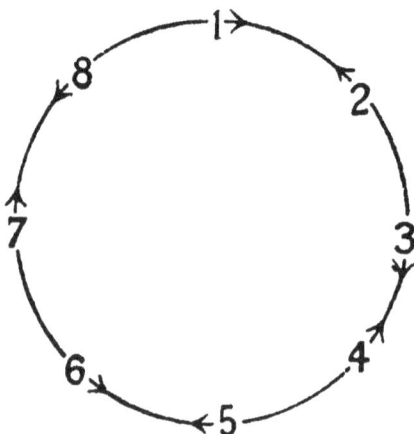

DIAGRAM A.

Odd numbers face and move round clockwise; even numbers counter-clockwise. All move at the same rate and, upon meeting, pass alternately by the right and left.

This progression is shown in diagram B, the dotted and unbroken lines indicating the tracks described, respectively, by odd and even numbers. It will be seen that in every circuit the two opposing groups of dancers, odd and even, thread through each other twice; that is, there will be eight simultaneous passings, or *changes*, as we will call them, in each complete circuit :—

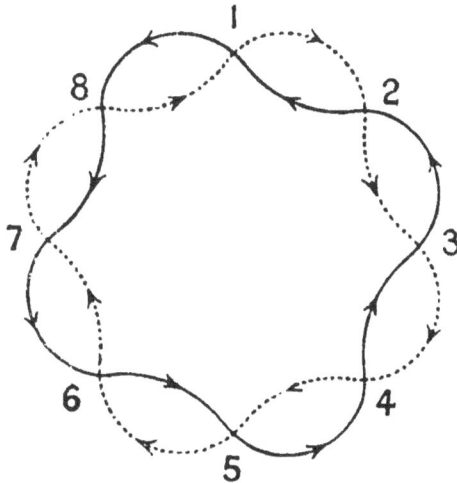

DIAGRAM B.

This movement is identical with that of the Grand Chain, except that in the familiar Lancers' figure the performers take hands, alternately right and left, as they pass; whereas, in the Country Dance hey, "handing," as Playford calls it, is the exception rather than the rule.

In this form the hey presents no difficulty. No misconception can arise so long as (1) the initial dispositions of the pairs, and (2) the duration of the movement, measured by circuits or changes, are clearly defined. And instructions on these two points will always be given in the notation. It should be understood that, in the absence of directions to the contrary, (1) the first pass is by the right, and (2) the dancers pass without handing.

FIGURE 19.

PROGRESSIVE CIRCULAR HEY.

Sometimes the hey is danced progressively, the dancers beginning and ending the movement pair by pair, instead of simultaneously, as above described. This is effected in the following way :—

The first change is performed by one pair only, say **Nos. 1 and 2** (see diagram A, Fig. 18); the second by two pairs, Nos. 1 and 3, and Nos. 2 and 8; the third, in like manner, by three pairs; and the fourth by four pairs. At the conclusion of the fourth change Nos. 1 and 2 will be face to face, each having traversed half a circuit, and all the dancers will be actively engaged, thus :—

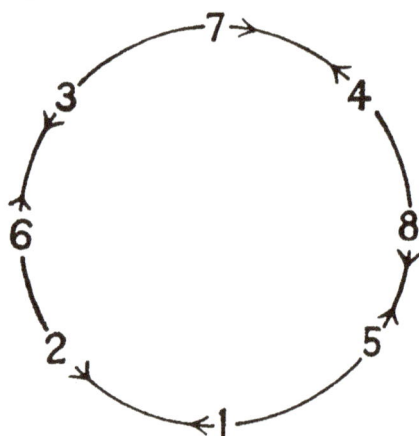

DIAGRAM C.

The movement now proceeds in the usual way. At the end of every complete circuit the position will be as follows :—

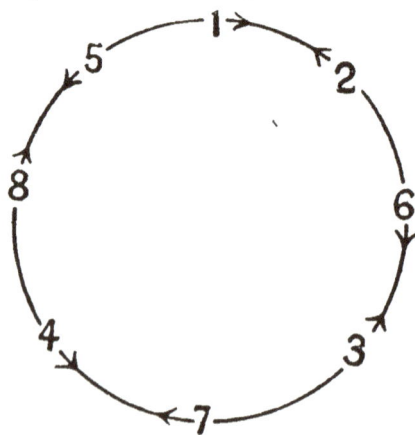

DIAGRAM D.

The figure is concluded in the following manner:—
Nos. 1 and 2, upon reaching their original places (see
diagram D), stop and remain neutral for the rest of the
movement. The others continue dancing until they reach
their proper places when they, in like manner, stop and
become neutral. This they will do, pair by pair, in the
following order, Nos. 3 and 8, 4 and 7, 5 and 6. The initial
and final movements thus occupy the same time, *i.e.*, four
changes.

Whenever the progressive hey occurs (1) the initial pair
will be named; and (2) the duration of the movement,
measured by changes or circuits, will be given in the notation.

FIGURE 20.

THE STRAIGHT HEY.

The dancers stand in a straight line at equi-distant stations,
alternately facing up and down, thus:—

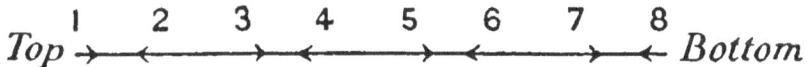

Top 1 2 3 4 5 6 7 8 *Bottom*

DIAGRAM E.

Odd numbers face down; even numbers up. As in the
circular hey the dancers move at an even rate, and pass each
other alternately by the right and left. The movement is
shown in diagram F, the dotted and unbroken lines indicating,
respectively, the upward and downward tracks described by
the dancers:—

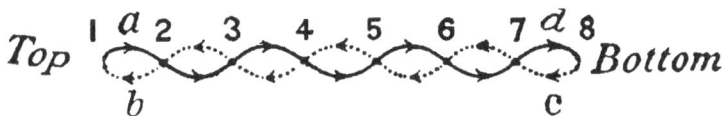

Top 1 *a* 2 3 4 5 6 7 *d* 8 *Bottom*
b   *c*

DIAGRAM F.

From this diagram it will be seen that the movements of
individual dancers are the same as those of the couples in a

progressive Country Dance (duple minor-set), with this difference—that the neutrals, instead of remaining passive, reverse their direction by moving round the loops *d c* or *b a*.

In the first change, all the dancers will be actively engaged, meeting and passing each other, and there will be no neutrals. But in the second change, there will be two neutrals, Nos. 2 and 7, both of whom will turn to their right and move, No. 2 round the loop *b a*, No. 7 round the loop *d c*. In the third change, Nos. 2 and 7, having reversed their directions, re-enter the track and all the dancers pass, in pairs, as in the first change. In this way the track is converted into an endless path and the continuous and characteristic rhythmic movement of the hey is preserved.

When, therefore, the number of dancers is even, as in the above example, there will be, in alternate rounds, (1) no neutrals, and (2) two neutrals, one at each end.

The distribution, however, will be somewhat different when the number of dancers is uneven, as the following diagram will show :—

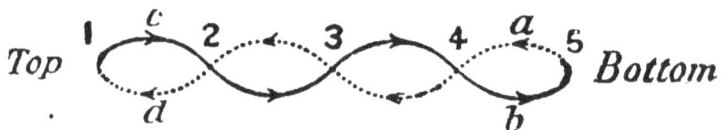

DIAGRAM G.

Odd numbers face down ; even numbers up. No.5, being neutral in the first change, will turn out to his left and move along the dotted line *a* preparatory to passing No. 3 by the left in the next change. In the second change, No. 2, being neutral at the upper end, will turn to his right and move round the loop *d c* and reverse his direction.

When this variation is performed by three dancers only, we have the form in which the hey occurs very frequently in the Country Dance. For this reason it will perhaps be advisable to describe this particular form in detail.

FIGURE 21.

THE HEY FOR THREE.

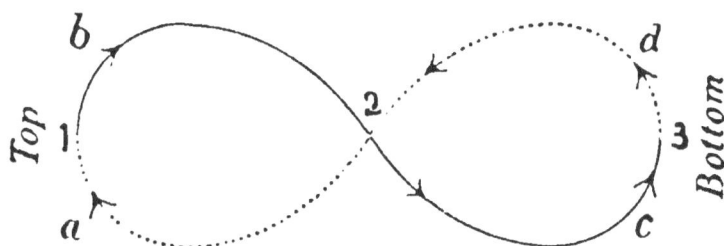

The movement is executed in six changes in the following way :—

> (1.) Nos. 1 and 2 face each other and pass by the right, No. 1 moving along the unbroken line, No. 2 along the dotted line ; while No. 3 faces up and gets ready to pass No. 1 by the left in the next change—and this he may do in two different ways, presently to be described.

> (2.) Nos. 1 and 3 pass by the left, No. 1 moving along the unbroken line, No. 3 along the dotted line ; while No. 2 reverses his direction by bearing to his right and moving round the top loop from *a* to *b*.

> (3.) Nos. 2 and 3 pass by the right, No. 2 moving along the unbroken line, No. 3 along the dotted line ; while No. 1 bears to his left, moves round the bottom loop from *c* to *d* and reverses his direction.

This completes the first half of the figure, called the *half-hey*. Nos. 1 and 3 have changed ends, while No. 2 is in his original station.

(4.) Nos. 1 and 2 pass by the left, No. 1 moving along the dotted line, No. 2 along the unbroken line ; while No. 3 bears to his right, moves round the top loop from *a* to *b* and reverses his direction.

(5.) Nos. 1 and 3 pass by the right, No. 1 along the dotted line, No. 3 along the unbroken line ; while No. 2 bears to his left, moves round the bottom loop from *c* to *d* and reverses his direction.

(6.) Nos. 2 and 3 pass by the left to places ; while No. 1 bears to his right and moves into his place.

This completes the figure—the *whole-hey*—and the dancers are once again in their original positions.

The nature of the preparatory movement made by No. 3 during the first change depends upon the initial disposition of the three dancers. If, for instance, the position is that of a longways dance for six, and all the dancers are facing front, No. 3's initial movement will depend upon the file to which he belongs. If on the men's side, he will merely move forward in a curve toward the middle of the General Set in preparation for the left-pass in the second change. If on the women's side, she will turn out to her left and cast up, bearing a little to her right, *i.e.*, outward and away from the General Set.

The above is presumably the correct way in which the hey-for-three should be executed in the Country Dance, although we have no direct evidence that it was in fact so danced in Playford's day. Hogarth, however, in his *Analysis of Beauty* (1753), after defining the hey as "a cypher of S's, a number of serpentine lines interlacing and intervolving one another," prints a diagram of the hey-for three which, although it might have been clearer, seems to show that the way the figure was danced at that period was substantially the same as that described above.

Moreover, Wilson (*The Analysis of Country Dancing*, 1811) also describes the figure and prints a diagram, of which the following—except that for clearness' sake the tracks are differentiated by means of varied lines—is a faithful reproduction :—

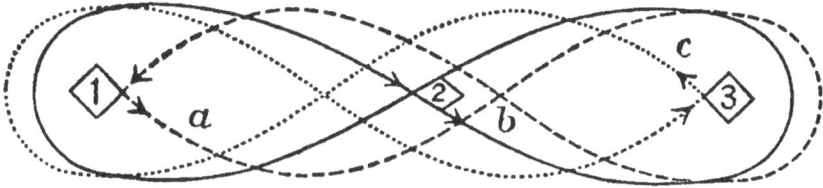

No. 1 moves along the broken line *a* ; No. 2 along the line *b* ; and No. 3 along the dotted line *c*.

Except that the two half-heys are inverted—the two *lower* dancers beginning the movement and passing by the *left*—the method shown in the diagram is precisely the same as that we have above described.

The straight-hey may be performed progressively. It is unnecessary, however, to describe in detail the way in which this is effected, because, in principle, the method is the same as that already explained in Fig. 19.

Playford makes frequent use of the expressions "Single Hey" and "Double Hey." It is difficult to say with certainty what he means by these terms, because he uses them very loosely. Very often they are identical with what we have called the straight- and circular-hey. As, however, this is not always the case, I have, with some reluctance, substituted the terms used in the text, which are self-explanatory and free from ambiguity.

GENERAL INSTRUCTIONS.

The preceding explanations of the steps, figures, etc., will, it is hoped, enable the reader to comprehend and to interpret the Notations which are now to follow. It should be remembered, however, that, although every movement be executed with scientific precision, this is but the first step toward the goal which every dancer should have in view. Technical proficiency, of itself, is of little worth. To the performer who is infected with the true spirit of the dance, technique is merely the vehicle of artistic expression.

Now the dominant characteristic of the English Country Dance is its " gay simplicity "—gaiety expressed by simple, easy, unaffected movements. Pointing the toe, arching the leg, affecting a swaying and mincing gait, all movements, indeed, devised to achieve a conventional elegance, are alien to the true spirit of this dance. Such devices are the stock-in-trade of the self-conscious dancer, ever mindful of his own appearance and the impression which he is making upon the onlookers. They are not the movements of those whose sole aim is self-expression, who dance for the joy of dancing and the rich opportunity it offers for the exercise of those emotional and imaginative faculties, for which, in the ordinary rough-and-tumble of everyday life, it is not easy to find an outlet. Affected movements are not bad only because they are ugly—though that may be reason enough— but primarily because they are self-conscious, self-consciousness being, of course, the arch-foe of all natural, instinctive, artistic expression.

Now, the English Country-Dance, prior at any rate to the 18th century, had never throughout its recorded history been used as a spectacle for the entertainment of others. It had always been danced for its own sake; for the purpose of self-expression, not self-glorification; as an art, not a pageant. And therein, of course, lies its unique value.

The technique of the Country-Dance is really a very simple one. The steps are all easy and natural, while the execution of the figures, even the most elaborate, presents but little difficulty when once the dancer has grasped the conception that motion is not so much a matter of the legs as of body-balance —a principle to which every traditional folk-dancer instinctively conforms. If the beginner will only seize this principle, leave his feet to take care of themselves,—remembering that they are supports, not ornaments,—always incline his body according to the direction of his motion, and concentrate his attention wholly upon the figures, he will soon acquire all the technique required of the Country Dancer.

Again, performers must never forget the intimate relationship which should always exist between the dance and the tune to which it is set. After all, the movements of the dance are but the interpretation or translation, in terms of bodily action, of the music upon which they are woven—just as the melody of a song is primarily the musical expression of the words to which it is wedded. For this reason, the dancer should carefully listen to the tune to which he is about to dance, assimilate it thoroughly and, if possible, commit it to memory. In particular, let him take careful note of its construction, *i.e.*, the number, character, and relative lengths of its several strains, in order that he may time and "phrase" his movements in accordance with them. The *tempo* of the dance should be determined by the character of its tune, that is, solely upon musical considerations. The application of this principle, viz., the subordination of the dance to the music, is absolutely imperative in the present case. For the Playford dances are very persistent in type, and, were it not for the wide range of the emotional content of the tunes, it would be extremely difficult to give to them the requisite variety of treatment.

Although style in the matter of art is intuitive rather than to be acquired by precept, a question of feeling, not of thought, and is altogether too subtle, elusive and intangible a thing to be captured and set down in words, the following maxims may, nevertheless, be of some help to the beginner, the more particularly if they be taken as suggestions rather than rules :—

(1.) Make no movement, however insignificant, that is not rhythmically in agreement with the music. For instance, in giving or taking a hand in the hey, or when "leading", begin the movement in plenty of time—two or more beats before hand—and take care to raise and move the arm in rhythm with the music.

(2.) When "leading", do not regard the taking of hands as a mere formality. The leader should actually lead—that is, guide and regulate the movements of his partner.

(3.) The Country-Dance is a concerted or group-dance. A large part of the enjoyment derived from country-dancing arises directly from the cultivation by the dancers of a communal feeling and understanding. This has, of course, its technical counterpart in the harmonizing of the movements of each individual with those of the other dancers—an art in itself, and one only acquired after much practice and experience.

(4.) Before beginning a figure from rest, make some preliminary rhythmical movement (akin to the "Once-to-yourself", or the preparatory jump made before each figure of the Morris Dance), so that you may start easily and naturally with the music. The purpose of "the two steps back", the initial movement of so many figures, is to give the dancer a rhythmical balance preparatory to the execution of the movement.

(5.) Remember that the dances in the Notations are divided into Parts, figures, etc., merely for the purpose of clear description. The aim of the dancer should be to conceal, not to call attention to these divisions; rather, perhaps, to regard the successive figures of a dance as the subordinate parts of a complete sentence, giving to each no more than its due emphasis.

(6.) The steps prescribed in the Notation are not obligatory. Nor is uniformity necessary, *i.e.*, that every dancer should use the same step at the same time; nor, again, that a single figure should always be danced to one step throughout —the arbitrary change of step in the course of a movement is not only permissible, but is in many cases to be commended.

(7.) In taking a step, be careful not to glide, *i.e.*, gradually to transfer the weight of the body from one foot to the other. Crawling is not dancing. The spring, however slight it may be—and it should always be as low as possible—is an essential element of every Country-Dance step.

NOTATION.

PUT ON THY SMOCK ON A MONDAY.

Round for six; in three parts (4th Ed. 1670).

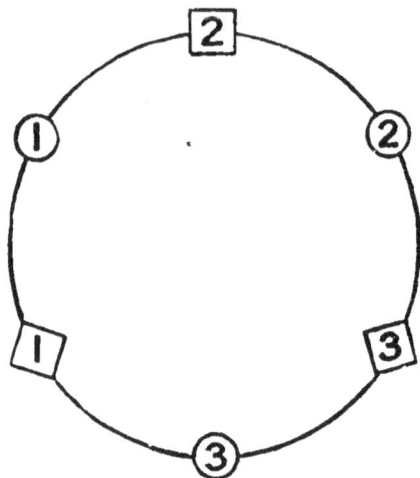

MUSIC.		MOVEMENTS.
		First Part.
A1	1—4	Hands-six, eight slips clockwise.
	5—8	Partners set and turn single.
A2	1—4	Hands-six, eight slips counter-clockwise to places.
	5—8	Partners set and turn single.
A3	1—4	First man leads first and second women forward a double towards third woman, and falls back a double (r.s.).
	5—8	First man turns third woman; while first and second women turn each other.
A4	1—8	As in A3, first man leading third and first women forward towards second woman, first man turning second woman, first and third women turning each other.

PUT ON THY SMOCK ON A MONDAY—*continued.*

MUSIC.		MOVEMENTS.
		FIRST PART—*continued.*
A5	1—8	As in A3, first man leading second and third women forward towards first woman, first man turning his partner, second and third women turning each other.
		SECOND PART.
A1	1—4	Sides all.
	5—8	Partners set and turn single.
A2	1—8	All that again.
A3, A4 and **A5**		As in First Part, second man doing as first man did.
		THIRD PART.
A1	1—4	Partners arm with the right.
	5—8	Partners set and turn single.
A2	1—4	Partners arm with the left.
	5—8	Partners set and turn single.
A3, A4 and **A5**		As in First Part, third man doing as first man did.

THE GELDING OF THE DEVIL.

Round for six ; in three parts (3rd Ed., 1665).

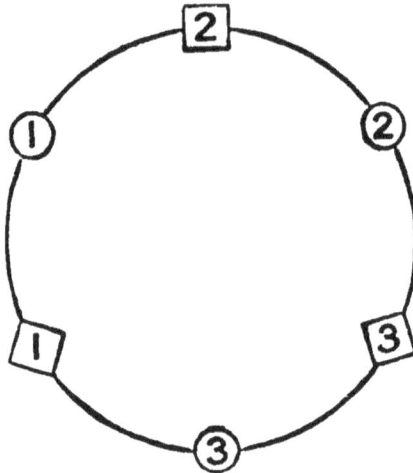

MUSIC.		MOVEMENTS.
		FIRST PART.
A	1—8	Hands-six, eight slips clockwise and eight slips counter-clockwise to places.
B1	1—4	First man and first woman lead forward a double and fall back a double to places (r.s.).
	5—8	Leading forward again (r.s.), they pass between second man and third woman and cast off (sk.s.) to places, the first man to his left outside second couple, and the first woman to her right outside third couple.
B2	1—8	As in B1, second couple leading forward and passing between first woman and third man.
B3	1—8	As in B1, third couple leading forward and passing between first man and second woman.

THE GELDING OF THE DEVIL—*continued.*

MUSIC.		MOVEMENTS.
		SECOND PART.
A	1—4	Sides all.
	5—8	That again.
B1, B2 and B3.		As in First Part.
		THIRD PART.
A	1—4	Partners arm with the right.
	5—8	Partners arm with the left.
B1, B2 and B3		As in First Part.

OAKEN LEAVES.

Round for eight; in three parts (4th Ed., 1670).

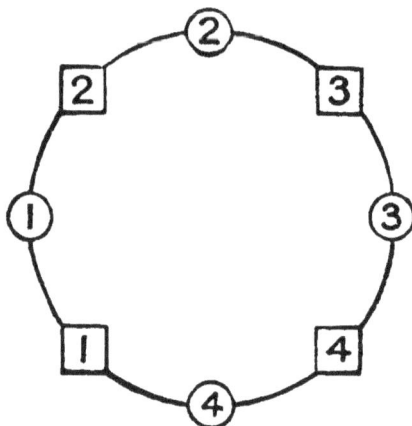

MUSIC.		MOVEMENTS.
		FIRST PART.
A1	1—4	Hands-all, eight slips clockwise.
	5—8	Partners set and turn single.
A2	1—4	Hands-all, eight slips counter-clockwise to places.
	5—8	Partners set and turn single.
A3	1—2	First and second men change places (r.s.).
	3—4	First and second women change places (r.s.).
	5—8	First and second couples circular-hey to places, two changes, partners facing.
A4	1—8	Third and fourth couples do likewise.
		N.B.—*This Part can, if desired, be made equal in length to each of the subsequent Parts, if the movements in A3 and A4 be repeated, respectively, by the first and fourth couples and by the second and third couples.*

OAKEN LEAVES—*continued.*

MUSIC.		MOVEMENTS.
		SECOND PART.
A1	1—4	Partners side.
	5—8	Partners set and turn single.
A2	1—8	All that again.
A3	1—4	Men lead out their partners a double, away from the centre, change hands, and lead them back again.
	5—	Men, passing in front of their partners, turn the next woman on their right once round.
A4, A5 and **A6**		Movement in A3 repeated three times to places, the men in each repetition leading out the women they have just turned.
		THIRD PART.
A1	1— 4	Partners arm with the right.
	5—8	Partners set and turn single.
A2	1—4	Partners arm with the left.
	5—8	Partners set and turn single.
A3	1—4	The men move forward a double to the centre and fall back a double to places.
	5—8	Each man turns the woman on his left once-and-a-half round, and moves into her partner's place.
A4, A5, and **A6.**		Movement in A3 repeated three times to places, the men in each repetition turning the women on their left and passing on, clockwise, into the next man's place.

SELLENGER'S ROUND; OR, THE BEGINNING OF THE WORLD.

Round for as many as will ; in four parts (4th Ed. 1670).

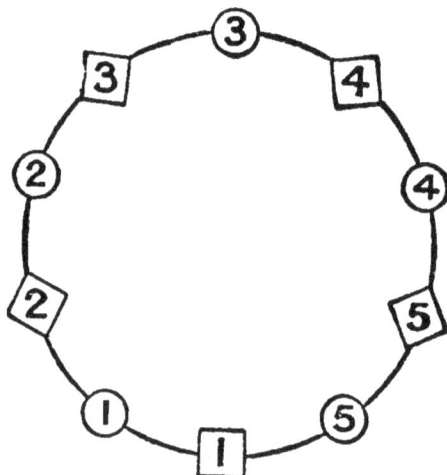

MUSIC.		MOVEMENTS.
		FIRST PART.
A.	1—8	Hands-all, eight slips clockwise and eight slips counter-clockwise to places.
B1	1—2	All move forward two singles toward the centre, beginning the first with the right foot, and the second with the left.
	3—4	All fall back a double to places.
	5—8	Partners set and turn single.
B2	1—8	All that again.

SELLENGER'S ROUND—*continued.*

MUSIC.	MOVEMENTS.
	SECOND PART.
A. 1—4	All take hands, move forward a double to the centre, and fall back a double to places.
5—8	That again.
B1 and **B2**	As in First Part.
	THIRD PART.
A. 1—4	Partners side.
5—8	That again.
B1 and **B2**	As in First Part.
	FOURTH PART.
A. 1—4	Partners arm with the right.
5—8	Partners arm with the left.
B1 and **B2**	As in First Part.

HEARTSEASE.

For four; in three parts (1st Ed. 1650).

2   ②

①   1

MUSIC.		MOVEMENTS.
		Running-step throughout the dance.
		First Part.
A	1—4	Couples move forward a double, meet, and fall back a double to places.
	5—8	That again.
B1	1—4	First man and second woman face down; first woman and second man face up. All fall back a double and move forward a double.
	5—8	First man and second woman turn with right hands and fall back to places; while second man and first woman do the same.
B2	1 4	All fall back a double and move forward a double to places.
	5—8	Partners turn with left hands.
		Second Part.
A	1—4	Partners side.
	5—8	Contraries side.
B1 and B2		As in First Part.
		Third Part.
A	1—4	Partners arm with the right.
	5—8	Contraries arm with the left.
B1 and B2		As in First Part.

HIT AND MISS.

For four ; in three parts (1st Ed. 1650).

$$\boxed{2} \quad \textcircled{2}$$

$$\textcircled{1} \quad \boxed{1}$$

MUSIC.		MOVEMENTS.
		Running-step throughout the dance.
		FIRST PART.
A	1—4	Couples move forward a double, meet, and fall back a double to places.
	5—8	That again.
B	1—2	Couples move forward a double and meet.
	3—4	First man leads second woman up a double, while second man leads first woman down a double.
	5—6	Both couples turn and face one another. First man leads second woman down a double ; while second man leads first woman up a double.
	7—8	First man and first woman, joining right hands, fall back a double to places ; while second man and second woman do the same.
C	1—6	Circular-hey, partners facing, four changes.
		SECOND PART.
A	1—4	Sides all.
	5—8	That again.
B and C		As in First Part.
		THIRD PART.
A	1—4	Partners arm with the right.
	5—8	Partners arm with the left.
B and C		As in First Part.

THE BOATMAN.

Longways for six; in three parts (1st Ed. 1650).

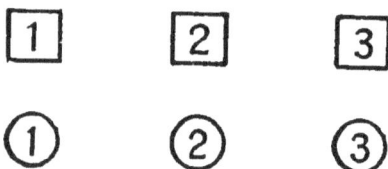

| 1 | 2 | 3 |

| ① | ② | ③ |

MUSIC.		MOVEMENTS.
		Running-step throughout the dance.
		FIRST PART.
A1	1—4	All lead up a double and fall back a double to places.
	5—8	Partners set and turn single.
A2	1—8	All that again.
B1	1—4	First couple and second man the straight-hey, four changes (the three standing in line, second man in the middle facing first woman and passing her by the right); while the third couple and second woman do the same (the latter facing third man and passing him by the right).
	5—8	Partners turn, the first and third couples once round, the second couple half-way round. *All are now in their opposite places.*
B2	1—4	As in B1, except that second man heys with third couple (facing third woman and passing her by the right) while second woman heys with first couple) (facing first man and passing him by the right).
	5—8	Partners turn as in B1, to places.

THE BOATMAN—*continued.*

MUSIC.		MOVEMENTS.
		SECOND PART.
A1	1—4	Sides all.
	5—8	Partners set and turn single.
A2	1—8	All that again.
B1	1—2	First couple and second man hands-three half-way round and stand in line facing down, second man in the middle ; while third couple and second woman do likewise and stand in line facing up, second woman in the middle.
	3—4	Still holding hands, all fall back two steps and move forward two steps.
	5—8	Second man and second woman meet in the middle of the Set, turn each other once-and-a-quarter round and fall into the middle station (improper) ; while first and third men turn their partners once round. *All are now in their opposite places.*
B2	1—2	As in B1, except that second man hands-three half-way round with third couple, second woman with first couple.
	3—8	As in B1, to places.

THE BOATMAN—*continued.*

MUSIC.		MOVEMENTS.
		THIRD PART.
A1	1— 4	Partners arm with the right.
	5—8	Partners set and turn single.
A2	1—4	Partners arm with the left.
	5—8	Partners set and turn single.
B1	1—4	First and third men and second woman hands-three round second man to places.
	5—8	Second man turns his partner.
B2	1— 4	First and third women and second man hands-three round second woman to places.
	5—8	Second man turns his partner.

THE WHIRLIGIG.

Longways for six ; in three parts (1st Ed. 1650).

MUSIC.		MOVEMENTS.
		First Part.
A1	1—4	All lead up a double and fall back a double to places.
	5—8	That again.
B1	1—4	Second man and second woman lead up the middle to the top, cast off and return to places.
	5—8	Second woman crosses over, passes counter-clockwise round first man and returns to her place ; while second man crosses over, passes clockwise round first woman and returns to his place (r.s.).
B2	1—4	Second man and second woman lead down the middle to the bottom, cast off and return to places.
	5—8	Second woman crosses over, passes clockwise round third man and returns to her place ; while second man crosses over, passes counter-clockwise round third woman and. returns to his place (r.s.).
A2	1—4	First man, followed by second and third men, casts off to the bottom ; while first woman, followed by second and third women, does the same (sk.s.).

THE WHIRLIGIG—*continued.*

MUSIC.	MOVEMENTS.
	FIRST PART—*continued.*
5—8	Second man and second woman, followed respectively by third man and third woman, lead down the middle, pass between first man and first woman, and cast off to the top, the men to their right, the women to their left (progressive) (sk.s.).
	The movements in B1, B2 and A2 are now repeated twice to places as in a progressive longways dance (Whole-set), the third couple occupying the middle position in the first repetition, and the first couple in the last.
	SECOND PART.
A1 1—4	Partners side.
5—8	That again.
B1 1—8	Second man crosses over, arms first woman with the right, and then goes the whole-hey with the first couple, second man facing first man and passing him by the *left.* Simultaneously, second woman arms third man with the right and goes the whole-hey with the third couple, second woman facing third woman and passing her by the *left* (r.s.).
B2 1—8	As in B1 to places, second man arming third man with the right and heying with the third couple ; second woman arming first woman and heying with the first couple.
A2 1—8	As in First Part (progressive).
	The movements in B1, B2 and A2 are now repeated twice progressively to places.

THE WHIRLIGIG—*continued.*

MUSIC.		MOVEMENTS.
		THIRD PART.
A1	1—4	Partners arm with the right.
	5—8	Partners arm with the left.
B1	1—4	First man, followed by second man, casts down into the second place, and returns up the middle to his own place ; while first woman, followed by second woman, does the same (r.s.).
	5—8	First and second couples right-hands across (r.s.).
B2	1—4	Third man and third woman, followed respectively by second man and second woman, cast up and return down the middle to places.
	5—8	Second and third couples right-hands-across.
A2	1—8	As in First Part (progressive).
		The movements in B1, B2 and A2 are now repeated twice progressively to places.

PICKING UP STICKS.

Longways for six ; in three parts (1st Ed. 1650).

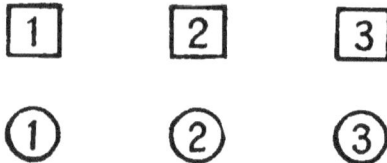

| 1 | 2 | 3 |
| (1) | (2) | (3) |

MUSIC.		MOVEMENTS.
		FIRST PART.
A1	1—4	All lead up a double and fall back a double to places.
	5—8	That again.
A2	1—4	First man changes places with the middle dancer on the opposite side and then with the last dancer on his own side (r.s.).
	5—8	All lead up a double and fall back a double to places.
A3	1—4	First woman does as first man did in A2.
	5—8	As in A2.
A4	1—4	Second woman does as first man did in A2.
	5—8	As in A2.
A5	1—4	Second man does as first man did in A2.
	5—8	As in A2.
A6	1—4	Third man does as first man did in A2.
	5—8	As in A2.
A7	1—4	Third woman does as first man did in A2.
	5—8	As in A2.

PICKING UP STICKS—*continued.*

MUSIC.		MOVEMENTS.
		SECOND PART.
A1	1—4	Sides all.
	5– 8	That again.
A2	1—8	First man and first woman face, take both hands, and go four slips down between second man and second woman ; while second man and second woman go four slips up into the top place (2 bars). Second man and second woman take both hands and slip down to places between first man and first woman ; while first man and first woman slip up to places (2 bars). First and second couples repeat these movements (4 bars). Simultaneously, third man and third woman cross over, cast up to the top, cross over again and cast down to places (sk.s).
A3	1—8	Third and second couples do as first and second couples did in A2, third couple first slipping up between second man and second woman ; while first man and first woman cross over, cast down to the bottom, cross over again and cast up to places.
		THIRD PART.
A1	1—4	Partners arm with the right.
	5—8	Partners arm with the left.

PICKING UP STICKS—*continued.*

MUSIC.	MOVEMENTS.
	THIRD PART—*continued.*
A2, A3, and **A4**	First man, followed by second and third men, crosses over and threads or heys through the three women (they standing still), passing outside first woman, inside second, and outside third. The first and second men, on reaching the third woman, pass, clockwise, completely round her and face up ; while the third man, instead of following second man round third woman, passes counter-clockwise completely round second woman and faces up, thus becoming the head of the file (sk.s.).
	Third man, followed by first and second men, then heys up to the top, the second man (now the hindermost), instead of following first man round first woman, passing counter-clockwise round second woman, and facing down.
	The three, now led by second man, then hey once again to the bottom, the first man (now the hindermost) passing counter-clockwise completely round second woman and facing up.
	Led by first man, the three, now in their proper order, hey up to the top, turn to their right, cast down to the bottom, and then move up to their respective places.
A5, A6, and **A7.**	The women do as the men did in **A2, A3,** and **A4.**

SCOTCH CAP.

Longways for six ; in three parts (1st Ed., 1650).

MUSIC.		MOVEMENTS.
		Running-step throughout the dance.
		FIRST PART.
A	1—4	All lead up a double and fall back a double to places.
	5—8	That again.
B1	1—4	First and second women and second and third men fall back two steps, cross over and change places, first woman with second man and second woman with third man.
	5—8	First man and third woman fall back two steps, cross over, and change places.
B2	1—8	All that again to places.
		SECOND PART.
A	1—4	Partners side.
	5—8	That again.
B1	1—4	The men take hands, fall back a double and move forward a double to places; while the women do the same.
	5—8	First & third men, first & third women, second man & second woman, arm with the right and fall back to places.
B2	1—4	As in B1.
	5—8	Partners turn.

SCOTCH CAP—*continued.*

MUSIC.		MOVEMENTS.
		THIRD PART.
A	1—4	Partners arm with the right.
	5--8	Partners arm with the left.
B1	1—2	The men go four slips up, while the women go four slips down, so that third man faces first woman.
	3—8	Progressive hey, handing, three changes, to places, third man and first woman beginning the movement. (*In the third and last change, second man turns his partner once round with the right hand, while first and third men turn their partners three-quarters round.*)
B2	1—8	Same movement as in B1, except that the men slip down and the women slip up, and that first man and third woman begin the progressive hey.

GREENWOOD.

Longways for six; in six parts (1st Ed. 1650).

①   2   ③

1   ②   3

MUSIC.		MOVEMENTS.
		FIRST PART.
A1	1—4	All facing front, move forward a double and fall back a double to places.
	5—8	Partners set and turn single.
A2	1—4	The second man leads the first and third women out a double, changes hands and leads them back a double to places; while the second woman does the same with the first and third men.
	5—8	Partners set and turn single.
A3	1—4	Second man sides with his partner; while first man sides with third man, and first woman with third woman.
	5—8	Partners set and turn single.
A4	1—4	First man sides with second woman, and second man with first woman; while third man sides with his partner.
	5—8	Partners set and turn single.
A5	1—4	Second man sides with third woman, and third man with second woman; while first man sides with his partner.
	5—8	Partners set and turn single.

GREENWOOD—*continued.*

MUSIC.		MOVEMENTS.
		SECOND PART.
A1 and **A2**		As in First Part.
A3 and **A4**		As in First Part, except that the dancers arm with the right instead of siding.
A5	1—8	As in First Part, except that the dancers arm with the left instead of siding.
		THIRD PART.
A1 and **A2**		As in First Part.
A3	1—4	Each file hands-three.
	5—8	Partners set and turn single.
A4	1—4	First couple and second man hands-three; while third couple and second woman do the same.
	5—8	Partners set and turn single.
A5	1—4	Third couple and second man hands-three; while first couple and second woman do the same.
	5—8	Partners set and turn single.
		FOURTH PART.
A1 and **A2**		As in First Part.
A3	1—8	Each file goes the whole-hey.
A4	1—8	First woman moves forward between first and second men and all three go the whole-hey, second man and first woman passing by the right.
		Simultaneously, third man moves forward between second and third women and all three go the whole-hey, third man and second woman passing by the right.

GREENWOOD—*continued.*

MUSIC.		MOVEMENTS.
		FOURTH PART—*continued.*
A5	1—8	First man moves forward between first and second women, and all three go the whole-hey, first man facing second woman and passing by the left.
		Simultaneously, third woman moves forward between second and third men, and all three go the whole-hey, third woman and second man facing and passing by the left.
		FIFTH PART.
A1 and **A2**		As in First Part.
A3 ·	1—4	The three men go hands-three round second woman.
	5—8	Partners set and turn single.
A4	1—4	The three women go hands-three round second man.
	5—8	Partners set and turn single.
		SIXTH PART.
A1 and **A2**		As in First Part.
A3	1—8	The second woman falling back, the three men go the whole-hey, second man moving between first and third men and passing the latter by the right.
A4	1—8	The second man falling back, the three women go the whole-hey, second woman moving between the first and third women and passing the former by the right.
A5 and **A6**		Same as A1 and A2 in First Part.

STEP STATELY.

Longways for three, five, seven or nine couples ; in three
parts (1st Ed. 1650).

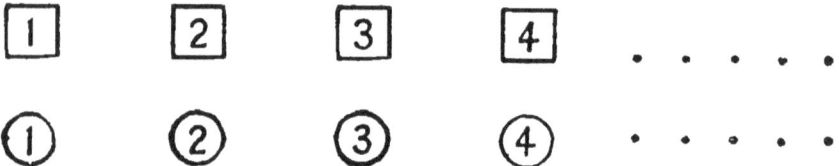

| 1 | 2 | 3 | 4 | . . . . . |
| ① | ② | ③ | ④ | . . . . . |

MUSIC.		MOVEMENTS.
		FIRST PART.
A	1—2	All lead up a double.
	3—4	Still facing up, men go four slips to their right behind their partners ; while the women go four slips to their left.
	5— 8	The men face the right wall and join hands, while the women face the left wall and do likewise. The first man, followed by the other men, casts down to the bottom of the Set and stands with the rest of the men in a straight line on his right hand, all facing the Presence ; while the women, in like manner, led by first woman, cast down and stand in line with the men, first woman next to first man.
B	1— 4	All take hands, move up a double and fall back a double.
	5—8	First man and first woman having released their hands, the women, hand-in-hand, move to the right in front of the men and dance up to places ; while the men move to the left and do the same.

STEP STATELY—*continued.*

MUSIC.		MOVEMENTS.
		SECOND PART.
		(Duple minor-set.)
A	1—4	First man and first woman lead up a double, change hands, and lead back to places.
	5—6	First and second couples hands-four half-way round (r.s.).
	7—8	First man and second woman change places.
B	1—4	First and second women lead up to the top, cross over and stand, the first woman behind the second man, the second woman behind the first man.
	5—8	The two men, giving right hands, pass each other, and then turn their partners with left hands, the first couple falling into the second place, the second couple into the first place (progressive) (sk.s.).
		THIRD PART.
		(Progressive.)
A	1—4	First man and first woman cross over, cast down and cross again in the second place, the second couple moving up to the top.
	5—6	The first three men taking hands, the first three women doing the same, all move forward a double, first man and first woman meeting, second and third men changing places with their partners.
	7—8	The two files fall back a double.
B	1—4	First man and first woman lead up to the top and then, followed by second couple, cast down into the third place, second couple falling into the second place, and third couple moving up into the first place.
	5—8	Second and third couples hands-four half-way round; while first man and first woman arm with the right (progressive)

STEP STATELY—*continued.*

*When three couples only are dancing, the progressive movement
is that of an ordinary Whole-set dance. When,
however, five, seven or nine couples are dancing, the
progressive movement is that of a triple minor-set
with this difference that the leading couples gain
two places in each round instead of one. In this
latter case, couples going up the dance should be
careful to note at the beginning of each round to
which minor-set they belong and their place in that
set. This they can most easily do by carefully noting
the positions and movements of the leading couples.
It should be noted that the restriction with regard to
the number of the performers is operative in the
Third Part only.*

AYE ME, OR, THE SYMPHONY.

Longways for eight ; in three parts (1st Ed. 1650).

| 1 | 2 | 3 | 4 |
| 1 | 2 | 3 | 4 |

MUSIC.		MOVEMENTS.
		Running-step throughout the dance.
		FIRST PART.
A1	1—4	Partners lead up a double and fall back a double to places.
	5—6	Partners face ; men fall back two steps in fifth bar, women the same in sixth bar.
	7—8	All move forward to places, turning single as they do so.
A2	1—8	All that again.
B1	1—4	First man and first woman cast down, meet below the second couple and change places ; while fourth man and fourth woman cast up, meet above the third couple and change places.
	5—8	First man and first woman cast up to the top, cross over and move down into the second place, the first man taking second man by both hands and turning him counter-clockwise up into the first place, the first woman in like manner turning second woman clockwise into the first place. Simultaneously, fourth and third couples do likewise.
B2	1—8	All that again to places, second and third couples initiating the movement.

AYE ME—*continued.*

MUSIC.		MOVEMENTS.
		SECOND PART.
A1	1—4	Partners honour (2 bars) and change places, passing by the *left* (2 bars).
	5 - 6	Men fall back two steps in fifth bar, women the same in sixth bar.
	7—8	All move forward a double to places, turning single as they do so.
A2	1—8	All that again to places.
B1	1—2	All face up. First and third men and women go four slips outward ; while second and fourth men and women go four slips inward.
	3 - 4	First and third couples fall back a double; while second and fourth couples move up a double.
	5—6	Still facing up, first and third men and women go four slips inward; while second and fourth men and women go four slips outward.
	7 - 8	First and third couples move forward a double ; while second and fourth couples fall back a double.
B2	1—2	As in B1, all facing down.
	3—4	First and third couples move forward a double ; while second and fourth couples fall back a double.
	5—6	As in B1, all facing down.
	7—8	First and third couples fall back a double to places ; while second and fourth couples move forward a double to places.

AYE ME—*continued.*

MUSIC.		MOVEMENTS.
		THIRD PART.
A1	1—4	Partners arm with the right once-and-a-half round, and change places.
	5—6	Men fall back two steps in fifth bar; the women doing the same in sixth bar.
	7—8	All move forward a double, turning single as they do so.
A2	1—4	Partners arm with the left once-and-a-half round to places.
	5—8	As in A1 to places.
B1	1—4	Second and third couples cast off and move into first and fourth places respectively. Simultaneously, first and fourth couples face, move forward, meet, change places (opposites passing by the right), and stay in the third and second stations respectively. Whereupon, first and fourth men change places with their partners.
	5—6	First man with his right hand takes the fourth man by the left and changes places with him, both moving counter-clockwise; while first woman with her left hand takes the fourth woman by the right and changes places with her, both moving clockwise.
	7—8	First and fourth men change places with their partners.
B2	1—8	Movement repeated to places, first and fourth couples casting off, while second and third couples meet, pass each other, etc

PRINCE RUPERT'S MARCH.
Longways for eight; in three parts (1st Ed. 1650).

| 1 | 2 | 3 | 4 |

| ① | ② | ③ | ④ |

MUSIC.	MOVEMENTS.
	Walking-step throughout the dance.
	FIRST PART.
A 1—8	First couple, followed by second, third and fourth couples, leads round to the right to the bottom and then up the middle to places.
B1 1—4	First man, followed by second, third and fourth men, crosses over, moves down outside the women and stands behind fourth woman.
5—6	All face left wall and move forward a double.
7—8	Men change places with the women opposite them.
B2 1—4	As in B1, fourth man leading the other men.
5—6	As in B1.
7—8	Partners change places.
	SECOND PART.
A 1—8	First couple, followed by the remaining three couples, leads round to the left to the bottom and then up the middle to places.
B1 and B2	The women do as the men did in the First Part, moving down behind the men, advancing toward the right wall, etc.

PRINCE RUPERT'S MARCH—*continued.*

MUSIC.		MOVEMENTS.
		THIRD PART.
A	1—8	As in First Part.
B1	1—4	The first man, followed by the other three men, crosses over and moves down to the bottom on the women's side; while the fourth woman, followed by the other three women, crosses over and moves up to the top on the men's side (*i.e.*, all move round clockwise).
	5—8	Partners face. All fall back a double and move forward a double.
B2	1—4	Movement in B1 repeated in reverse, the men headed by fourth man, the women headed by first woman moving down and up respectively to places (*i.e.*, all moving round counter-clockwise).
	5—8	As in B1.

THE HEALTH; OR, THE MERRY WASSAIL.

Longways for eight; in three parts (1st Ed. 1650).

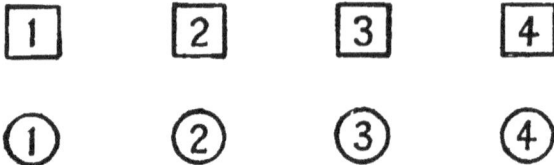

| 1 | 2 | 3 | 4 |

| ① | ② | ③ | ④ |

MUSIC.		MOVEMENTS.
		FIRST PART.
A1	1—4	All lead up a double and fall back a double to places.
	5—8	Partners set-and-honour.
A2	1—8	All that again.
A3	1—4	First and fourth couples face each other, meet and go back-to-back, staying in the second and third places respectively; while second couple casts up into the first place, and third couple casts down into the fourth place (r.s.).
	5—8	First man and first woman cast up to the top, and return down the middle to the same places; while fourth man and fourth woman cast down to the bottom, and return up the middle to the same places (r.s.).
A4	1—8	Movement repeated to places, second and third couples meeting, going back-to-back, etc.

THE HEALTH—*continued.*

MUSIC.		MOVEMENTS.
		SECOND PART.
A1	1— 4	Hands-all, half-way round, facing outward (r.s.).
	5—8	Partners set-and-honour.
A2	1—4	Hands-all, half-way round, counter-clockwise, facing outward to places (r.s.).
	5—8	Partners set-and-honour.
A3	1—4	As in A3, First Part.
	5—8	First and fourth couples hands-four, facing outward (r.s.).
A4	1—8	As in A3, second and third couples meeting, going back-to-back, etc.
		THIRD PART.
A1	1—4	Partners turn once-and-a-half round and change places (sk.s.).
	5— 6	First and second men, third and fourth men, first and second women, and third and fourth women turn half-way round and change places (sk.s.).
	7—8	Partners set.
A2	1—8	All that again to places.

THE HEALTH—*continued.*

MUSIC.		MOVEMENTS.
		THIRD PART—*continued.*
A3	1—4	First and fourth couples face each other and meet ; while second and third couples cast up and down respectively into first and fourth places (r.s.).
	5—8	First and fourth men and women clap their hands and go right-hands-across.
A4	1—8	Movement repeated to places, second and third couples meeting, clapping hands, etc.
		Alternative Version.
A3	1—2	First man and fourth woman move forward, meet and join right hands ; while second man casts up into first place and third woman casts down into fourth place (r.s.).
	3—4	First woman and fourth man move forward, meet and join right hands ; while second woman casts up into first place and third man casts down into fourth place.
	5—8	First and fourth couples right-hands-across once round.
A4	1—8	Movement continued to places, second man and third woman meeting, joining hands, etc.

HALFE HANNIKIN.

Longways for as many as will; in one part (1st Ed. 1650).

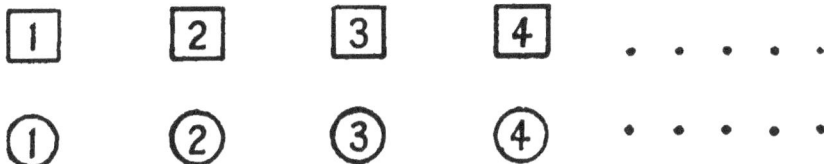

| 1 | 2 | 3 | 4 | . . . . . |
| ① | ② | ③ | ④ | . . . . . |

MUSIC.		MOVEMENTS.
		(Progressive.)
A	1—4	All lead up a double and fall back a double to places.
	5—8	That again.
B1	1—4	Opposites side.
	5—8	The top dancer on the men's side and the bottom dancer on the women's side turn their opposites and then fall out, the former standing neutral at the top, and on the right of the General Set, the latter at the bottom and on the left; while the rest of the dancers on the men's side turn their opposites and move up one place.
		All (with the exception of the two neutral dancers) are now facing up in couples, second man with first woman, third man with second woman, and so forth.
A2	1—4	All the couples lead up a double and fall back a double to places.
	5—8	That again.
B2	1—4	Opposites side.

HALFE HANNIKIN—*continued.*

MUSIC.	MOVEMENTS.
5—8	All the dancers on the women's side turn their opposites and move down one place, the neutral dancer at the top moving into the vacant place at the top of the women's side, and the neutral dancer at the bottom into the vacant place at the bottom of the men's side (progressive).
	The above movements are then repeated, and the dance proceeds until all the men have changed over to the women's side (first man at the lower end), and all the women have changed over to the men's side (last woman at the upper end) : or, if preferred, until all are once again in their original places.

THE COLLIER'S DAUGHTER; or, THE DUKE OF RUTLAND'S DELIGHT.

Longways for as many as will; in one part (Vol. 2,
4th Ed. 1728).

1	2	3	4	. . . .
①	②	③	④	. . . .

MUSIC.		MOVEMENTS.
		(Triple minor-set.)
A1	1—4	First man and first woman cross over and cast down into second place (improper), second couple moving up into first place.
	5—8	First man turns first woman.
A2	1—4	First man and first woman cross over and cast down into the third place (proper), third couple moving up into the second place.
	5—8	First man turns first woman.
B1	1—2	First man leads first woman up the middle into the second place, third couple moving down into the third place (progressive).
	3—6	First and second couples hands-four.
	7—8	All four turn single.
B2	1—4	First and second couples circular-hey, four changes, partners facing.
	5—8	First and second men turn their partners.

UP GOES ELY.

Longways for as many as will; in one part (Vol 3, *c.* 1728).

MUSIC.		MOVEMENTS.
		N.B.—*The tune is in triple time, i.e., three steps to the bar.*
		Running-step throughout the dance.
		(Triple minor-set.)
A	1—4	First man and first woman cast off into the second place (second couple moving up into the first place), turn each other half-way round and change places (improper), cast off again and meet below the third couple.
	5—8	First man and first woman lead up the middle to the top and cast off into the second place (still improper).
B	1—2	First man moves into the middle and, facing down, goes hands-three with the third couple half-way round; while first woman, facing up, does the same with the second couple.
		Second and third men have now changed places with their partners; while first woman is standing above the second couple, facing down, and first man below the third couple, facing up.
	3 – 4	First man and first woman meet, turn half-way round and fall back, each into the other's place.

UP GOES ELY—*continued.*

MUSIC.	MOVEMENTS.
5—6	First man (standing above second couple, facing down) goes hands-three with second couple half-way round ; while first woman (standing below third couple, facing up) does the same with third couple.
7—8	Second and third men turn their partners ; while first man and first woman face, turn three-quarters round and fall into the second place (progressive ; proper).

EVERY LAD HIS LASS.

Longways for as many as will; in one part
(Vol. 2, 4th Ed. 1728).

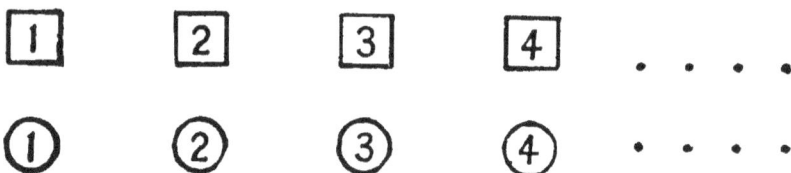

MUSIC.		MOVEMENTS.
		(Triple minor-set.)
A	1—4	First man and first woman set and cast down into second place, second couple moving up into first place.
	5—8	Second couple set and cast down into second place, first couple moving up into first place.
B	1—2	First man and second woman meet with two steps and a jump on the two beats of the first bar and the first beat of the second, respectively.
	3—4	First woman and second man meet in like manner.
	5—6	All four return to places, turning single as they do so.
	7—12	First man and first woman cross over, cast down, meet below second couple, cross over again, cast down, meet below third couple, and move up the middle into the second place; while second couple moves up into first place (progressive).

EPSOM NEW WELLS.

Longways for as many as will; in one part
(Vol. 2, 4th Ed. 1728).

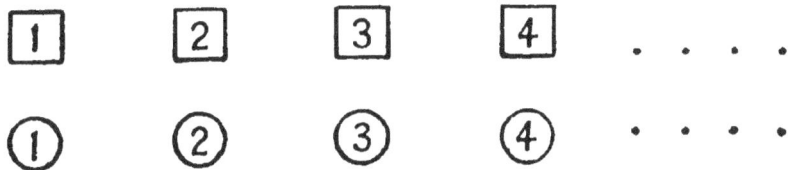

1   2   3   4   . . . .

①   ②   ③   ④   . . . .

MUSIC.		MOVEMENTS.
		(Triple minor-set.)
A	1—4	First man turns second woman half-way round. First man then passes clockwise round second man and returns to his place; while second woman passes clockwise round first woman and returns to her place.
	5—8	First woman turns second man half-way round. First woman then passes clockwise round first man and returns to her place; while second man passes clockwise round second woman and returns to his place.
B1	1—8	First man and first woman lead down the middle, while second man and second woman cast up and then follow behind them. First and second couples lead through the third couple, cast up, men to their right and women to their left, and return to places.
B2	1—4	First and second men lead a double to the left wall, change hands, and lead a double back again to places; while first and second women lead to the right wall and back again in like manner.
	5—6	Partners set.
	7—8	First man and first woman cast down into second place, second couple moving up into first place (progressive).

MY LADY'S COURANT.

Longways for as many as will; in one part
(Vol. 2, 4th Ed. 1728).

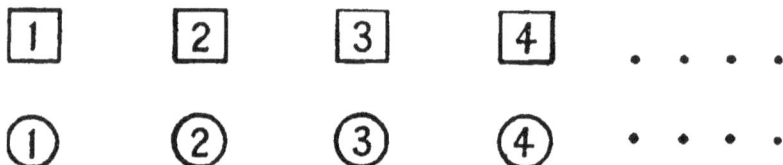

| 1 | 2 | 3 | 4 | . . . . |
| (1) | (2) | (3) | (4) | . . . . |

MUSIC.		MOVEMENTS.
		(Triple minor-set.)
A1	1—4	First man and first woman cast down into the second place, second couple moving up into first place.
	5—8	Second couple and first man hands-three once round, while third couple and first woman do the same.
A2	1—8	First man and first woman cast up to the top, cross over, cast down and hands-three once round, the man with second and third women, the woman with second and third men. *The first couple is now in the second place (improper).*
B1	1—4	First woman moves up the middle and passes clockwise round second woman to the second place on her own side; while first man moves up the middle and passes counter-clockwise round second man to the second place on his own side.

MY LADY'S COURANT—*continued.*

MUSIC.	MOVEMENTS.
5—8	First man and first woman turn each other and then cast up into the first place, second couple moving down into the second place.
B2 1—6	First man, taking his partner's left hand in his right—she taking the second woman's left hand in her right—casts off to his left, and, followed by first and second women, goes a complete circle, counter-clockwise, round second man.
7—8	First man and first woman cast down into the second place, second couple moving up into the first place (progressive).

ORLEANS BAFFLED.

Longways for as many as will; in one part
(Vol. 2, 4th Ed. 1728).

| 1 | 2 | 3 | 4 | . . . . |
| ① | ② | ③ | ④ | . . . . |

MUSIC.		MOVEMENTS.
		N.B.—*The tune is in triple time, i.e., three steps to the bar.*
		Running-step throughout the dance.
		(Triple minor-set.)
A	1—2	First man and first woman cast down into second place, second couple moving up into first place.
	3—4	First and third couples half-poussette and change places (first man pushing and then pulling).
	5—6	First man and first woman cast up into second place, third couple moving down into the third place.
	7—8	First and second couples half-poussette and change places (first man pulling and then pushing).
	Bar 9	First man and second woman change places.
	Bar 10	Second man and first woman change places.
	11—12	First and second couples circular-hey, three changes, men facing and women facing (progressive).

A TRIP TO KILBURN.

Longways for as many as will; in one part
(Vol. 2, 4th Ed. 1728).

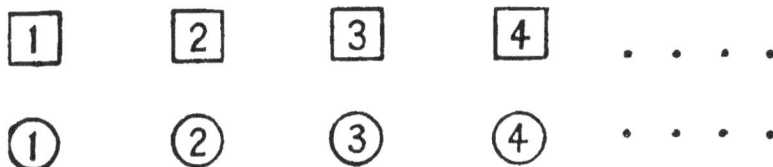

| 1 | 2 | 3 | 4 | · · · · |
| ① | ② | ③ | ④ | · · · · |

MUSIC.		MOVEMENTS.
		(Triple minor-set.)
A1	1—2	First man and first woman cast down into second place, second couple moving up into first place.
	3—6	First and third couples hands-four.
	7—8	First couple leads through third couple.
A2	1—2	First man and first woman cast up into the second place.
	3—6	First and second couples hands-four.
	7—8	First couple leads through second couple.
B1	1—2	First man and first woman cast off into second place (progressive).
	3—8	First, second and third couples hands-six.
B2	1—4	First and second couples circular-hey, four changes, partners facing.
	5—8	First and second men turn their partners.

MY LADY WINWOOD'S MAGGOT.

Longways for as many as will; in one part
(Vol. 3, *c.* 1728).

1	2	3	4	. . . .
①	②	③	④	· · · ·

MUSIC.		MOVEMENTS.
		(Triple minor-set.)
A1	1—4	First man and first woman set and cast down into second place, second couple moving up into first place.
	5—8	First man and first woman lead through the third couple and cast up into second place (progressive).
A2	1—8	First man goes figure of eight with third couple, passing counter-clockwise round the third woman and clockwise round the third man; while first woman does the same with second couple, passing counter-clockwise round second man and clockwise round second woman (sk.s.).
B1	1—4	First, second and third couples hands-six.
	5—8	First, second and third men go back-to-back with their partners.
B2	1—4	First man and first woman lead down through third couple, cast up to the top and lead down the middle to the second place.
	5—8	First man turns his partner.

THE MAIDEN'S BLUSH.

Longways for as many as will; in one part
(Vol. 2, 4th Ed. 1728).

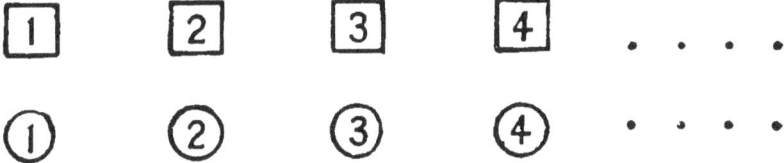

MUSIC.		MOVEMENTS.
		(Triple minor-set.)
A	1—4	First man and first woman set and cast down into second place, second couple moving up into first place.
	5—8	Same again, first couple changing places with third couple.
B1	1—4	First man and first woman lead up to the top, and cast down into second place, third couple moving down into third place.
	5—8	First and second couples circular-hey, two changes, partners facing.
B2	1—4	First and second men turn their partners.
	5—8	First and second couples circular-hey, two changes, partners facing (progressive).

JENNY, COME TIE MY CRAVAT.

Longways for as many as will; in two parts (8th Ed. 1690)

| 1 | 2 | 3 | 4 | . . . . |
| ① | ② | ③ | ④ | • • • • |

MUSIC.		MOVEMENTS.
		FIRST PART.
		(Triple minor-set.)
A	1—4	First man turns second woman.
	5—8	First woman turns second man.
B	1—8	First man and first woman cross over, cast down, cross over below the second couple, cast down again, meet below the third couple, lead up the middle to the top, and cast down into second place, second couple moving up into first place (progressive).
		SECOND PART.
		(Duple minor-set.)
A	1—2	First and second women fall back a double, while first and second men move forward a double.
	3—4	All four turn single.

JENNY, COME TIE MY CRAVAT—*continued.*

MUSIC.		MOVEMENTS.
		SECOND PART—*continued.*
	5— 6	The two men fall back a double, and the two women move forward a double to places.
	7—8	All four turn single.
B	1 - 4	Partners side, all clapping their hands on the first beat of the first bar.
	5—6	All four turn single.
	7—8	First man and first woman cast down into second place, while second couple moves up into first place, partners striking each other's hands (right on left and left on right) on the first beat of the bar (progressive).

MR. ISAAC'S MAGGOT.

Longways for as many as will; in one part (9th Ed. 1695).

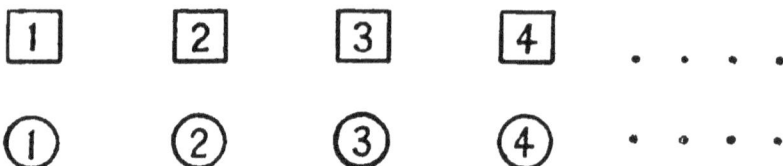

| 1 | 2 | 3 | 4 | . . . . |

| ① | ② | ③ | ④ | . . . . |

MUSIC.	MOVEMENTS.
	N.B.—*The tune is in triple-time; i.e., three steps to the bar.*
	(Duple minor-set.)
A 1—4	First man turns second woman with the right hand and returns clockwise round second man to his place.
5—8	First woman turns second man with the left hand and returns counter-clockwise round second woman to her place.
B 1—4	First and second men take hands, fall back six steps and move forward to places, turning single in the last three steps as they do so ; while first and second women do the same.
5—8	First and second couples circular-hey to places, four changes, partners facing. After the last change first man and first woman fall back and stand between second man and second woman, all four facing up.
9—10	First and second couples, four abreast, with linked hands, lead up three steps and fall back three steps.
11—12	First and second couple lead up three steps, the second couple staying in the first place, while first man and first woman cast down into the second place (progressive).

THE FIT'S COME ON ME NOW.

Longways for as many as will ; in one part (7th Ed. 1686).

MUSIC.		MOVEMENTS.
		N.B.—*The tune is in triple time, i.e., three steps to the bar.*
		(Duple minor-set.)
A	1—2	First man casts down, passes below second man and returns up the middle to his place ; while the second woman moves up the middle, casts down and returns to her place.
	3—4	First and second men turn their partners.
	5—6	First woman casts down, passes below the second woman and returns up the middle to her place ; while the second man moves up the middle, casts down and returns to his place.
	7—8	First and second men turn their partners.
B	Bar 1	First and second men change places with their partners.
	2—4	First woman and first man cross over and move down between second couple, cast up to their original places, and turn single.
	Bar 5	Second man and second woman cast up to the first place (improper), first couple moving down to second place (progressive).
	6—8	Second man and second woman cross over and move down between first couple, cast up into the first place, and turn single.

THE CORONATION DAY.

Longways for as many as will ; in one part
(10th Ed. 1698).

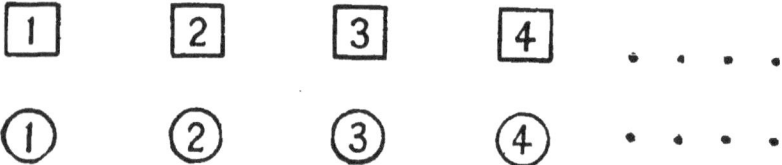

| 1 | 2 | 3 | 4 | . . . . |
| 1 | 2 | 3 | 4 | . . . . |

MUSIC.		MOVEMENTS.
		(Duple minor-set.)
A	1—4	First man with his right hand takes his partner by her left hand and leads her down the middle, passing her before him into second man's place, he falling into second woman's place; while second man and second woman cast up to the top, cross over and change sides.
	5—8	Second man with his left hand takes his partner by her right hand, and leads her down the middle into the second place, passing her before him on to her own side ; while first man and first woman cast up to the top, cross over and change sides.
B1	1—4	First man moves round his partner counter-clockwise into her place, while she (in bars 3 and 4) moves down into second woman's place, turning single as she does so. Simultaneously, second woman passes counter-clockwise round her partner into his place, while he (in bars 3 and 4) moves up into first man's place, turning single. clockwise, as he does so.

THE CORONATION DAY.—*continued.*

MUSIC.		MOVEMENTS.
	5—8	First man and first woman lead to the left wall between second man and second woman, cast off and return to the same places.
B2	1—2	Second man casts down and crosses over into the second place on the women's side ; while first woman crosses over into the first place on the men's side.
	3—4	All four turn single.
	5—8	First man and first woman cross over and cast down into the second place ; while second man with his right hand takes his partner by her left hand and leads her up the middle, passing her before him into the first place on the women's side, he falling into the first place on the men's side (progressive).

LADY BANBURY'S HORNPIPE.

Longways for as many as will; in three parts (3rd Ed. 1665).

| 1 | 2 | 3 | 4 | . . . . |

| (1) | (2) | (3) | (4) | . . . . |

MUSIC.	MOVEMENTS.
	N.B.—*The tune is in triple time, i.e., three steps to the bar.*
	FIRST PART.
	(Duple minor-set.)
A 1—4	First man and first woman cast down into the second place, cross over and stand, first man on the outside of second woman (both facing down), first woman on the outside of second man (both facing up).
B 1—2	First man and second woman (taking inside hands) lead down three steps and fall back three steps; while second man and first woman (taking inside hands) lead up three steps and fall back three steps.
3—4	Second man and second woman go right-hands-across half-way round, holding first woman and first man respectively in their left hands. Upon the conclusion of this movement, first couple falls into second place, while second man changes places with second woman and both fall into the first place (progressive).

* Playford bars it, wrongly, as we believe, in duple time.

LADY BANBURY'S HORNPIPE— *continued.*

MUSIC.		MOVEMENTS.
		SECOND PART.
		(Duple minor-set.)
A	1—2	The two men face and take both hands, the two women doing the same. First man pulls second man up three steps and pushes him down the middle three steps; while the second woman pulls first woman down three steps and then pushes her up the middle three steps. *All four are now in line, second man and first woman back to back.*
	3—4	First man and second woman change places, both moving to their left, *i.e.*, clockwise.
B	1—2	Second man and first woman go three slips to their left—second man toward left wall, first woman toward right wall. Whereupon second woman and first man change places.
	3—4	First and second couples hands-across rather less than half-way round (three steps), and partners change places (progressive).
		THIRD PART.
		(Duple minor-set.)
A	Bar 1	First man moves forward and stands above his partner, both facing up.

LADY BANBURY'S HORNPIPE—*continued.*

MUSIC.	MOVEMENTS.
	THIRD PART—*continued.*
Bar 2	Second man in like manner moves in front of his partner.
3—4	All four move up three steps and fall back three steps (w.s.).
B Bar 1	The first man goes three slips to his right, while his partner goes three slips to her left.
Bar 2	Second man and second woman do the same.
Bar 3	First man and first woman cast down into the second place, second couple leading up into the first place.
Bar 4	First and second men change places with their partners (progressive).

CHRISTCHURCH BELLS.

Longways for as many as will; in one part
(7th Ed. 1686).

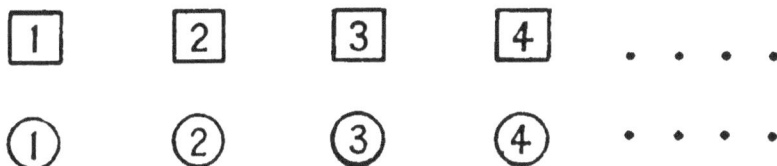

| 1 | 2 | 3 | 4 | . . . . |
| (1) | (2) | (3) | (4) | . . . . |

MUSIC.		MOVEMENTS.
		(Duple minor-set.)
A	1—8	First man turns second woman with the right hand and then turns his partner with the left, falling back into his place.
B	1—8	Second man turns first woman with the left hand and then turns his partner with the right, falling back into his place.
C	1—4	First and second couples hands-four.
	Bar 5	On the first beat of the bar, all clap hands; on the middle beat of the bar, partners strike right hands together.
	Bar 6	As in previous bar, except that, on the middle beat of the bar, partners strike left hands together.
	7—8	First man and first woman cast down into second place; while second couple leads up into first place (progressive).

THE WHIM.

Longways for as many as will; in one part
(9th Ed. 1695).

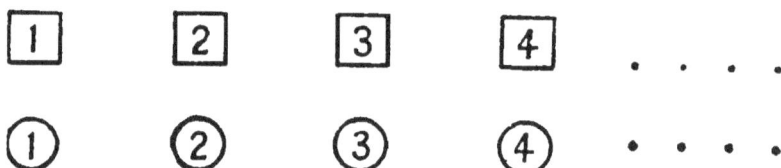

| 1 | 2 | 3 | 4 | . . . . |
| ① | ② | ③ | ④ | • • • • |

	MUSIC.	MOVEMENTS.
		(Duple minor-set.)
A	1—2	First and second men take hands and fall back a double; while first and second women do the same.
	3—6	Releasing hands, all four move forward, cross over, and change sides.
	7—12	Same again to places.
B	1—4	First and second men go back-to-back, while first and second women do the same.
	5—6	All four turn single.
	7—12	Circular-hey, three changes, partners facing, the first couple falling into the second place, the second couple into the first (progressive).

LOVE LIES A-BLEEDING.

Longways for as many as will; in one part (7th Ed. 1686).

1	2	3	4	• • • •
①	②	③	④	• • • •

MUSIC.		MOVEMENTS.
		(Duple minor-set.)
A	1—4	First man and first woman cast down into the second place, and then go back-to-back, passing by the right; while second couple moves up into the first place.
	5—8	First man and first woman cast up into the first place and then go back-to-back, passing by the left; while second couple moves down into the second place.
B	Bar 1	On the first beat of the bar, first and second men clap hands and, on the middle beat, strike each other's hands (right on left and left on right); while the two women do the same.
	Bar 2	As in previous bar, except that, on the middle beat, *partners* strike each other's hands.
	3—4	First man and first woman cast down into the second place, second couple moving up into the first place (progressive).
	5—6	As in bars 1—2.
	7—8	Partners turn each other.

JACOB HALL'S JIG.

Longways for as many as will; in one part (9th Ed. 1695).

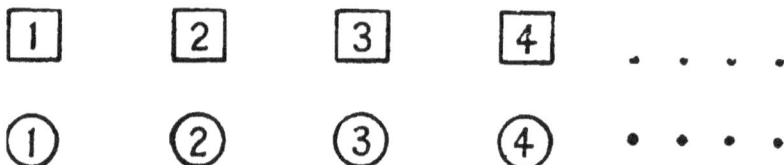

1	2	3	4	. . . .
①	②	③	④	• • • •

MUSIC.		MOVEMENTS.
		(Duple minor-set.)
A1	1—4	First man turns second woman with the right hand and then turns his partner with the left.
	5—8	First couple and second woman hands-three, counter-clockwise, to places.
A2	1—4	Second man turns first woman with the left hand and then turns his partner with the right.
	5—8	Second couple and first woman hands-three, clockwise, to places.
B1	1—4	First man and first woman lead down the middle, change hands, lead up and stand between second man and second woman, all four facing up.
	5—8	Taking hands, all four move up a double and fall back a double, first couple into second place, second couple into first place (progressive).
B2	1—4	First and second couples hands-four.
	5—8	First man and first woman lead up the middle, and cast down into second place.

THE TEMPLE CHANGE.

Longways for as many as will; in one part
(Vol. 2, 2nd Ed. 1698).

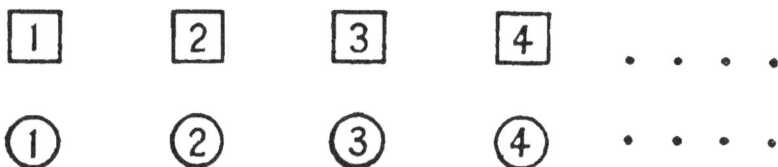

1	2	3	4	. . . .
①	②	③	④	• • • •

MUSIC.		MOVEMENTS.
		(Duple minor-set.)
A	1—2	First and second couples hands four half-way round.
	3—4	All turn single.
	5—8	All that again.
B	1—2	First man and second woman change places.
	3—4	First woman and second man change places.
	5—6	Hands-four half-way round.
	7—8	First man and first woman cast down into second place, the second couple leading up into first place (progressive).

THE MARY AND DOROTHY.

Longways for as many as will; in one part
(Vol. 3, c. 1728).

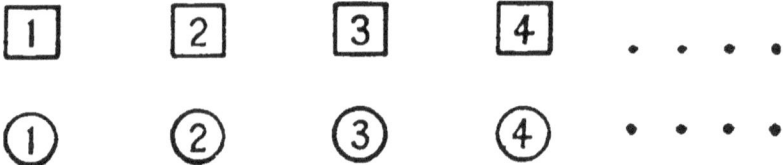

MUSIC.		MOVEMENTS.
		(Duple minor-set.)
A	1—4	First and second couples set and turn single.
	5—8	First and second couples hands-four.
B	1—4	First man leads first woman a double down the middle, changes hands, and leads her a double up.
	5—6	First man and first woman cast down into second place, second couple moving up into first place (progressive).

JOG ON.

Longways for as many as will; in four parts
(1st Ed. 1650).

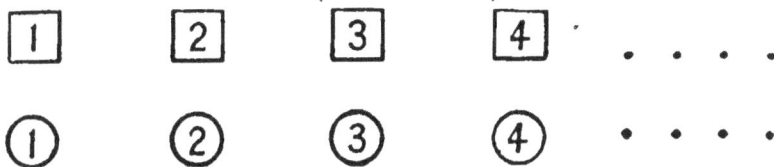

| 1 | 2 | 3 | 4 | · | . | . | . | . |

| ① | ② | ③ | ④ | • | • | . | • |

MUSIC.		MOVEMENTS.
		FIRST PART.
A1	1—4	All lead up a double and fall back a double to places.
	5—8	Partners set and turn single.
A2	1 – 8	All that again.
		SECOND PART. (Duple minor-set.)
A	1—4	First man, with his back to the Presence, faces his partner and, taking her by both hands, falls back two steps and then pushes her down the middle between second man and second woman.
	5—8	First man and second couple hands-three round first woman (first man standing on the right of second man), first couple falling into second place, second couple into first place (progressive).
		THIRD PART. (Duple minor-set.)
A	1—4	First man takes first woman by both hands, pushes her down behind second woman, and then into second man's place, he moving into second woman's place; while second couple moves up into the first place (progressive, improper).
	5 – 8	First and second men turn their partners.
		In the next round, first man pushes his partner behind third man into third woman's place (progressive, proper).

JOG ON—*continued.*

MUSIC.	MOVEMENTS.
	FOURTH PART.
A　1—4	First man and first woman cast down and stand on the outside of second man and second woman respectively, all four facing up. Taking hands, all move up a double and fall back a double, the first couple into the second place, the second couple into the first (progressive).
5—8	First and second men arm their partners with the right.

THE MOCK HOBBY HORSE.

Longways for as many as will; in one part
(10th Ed. 1698).

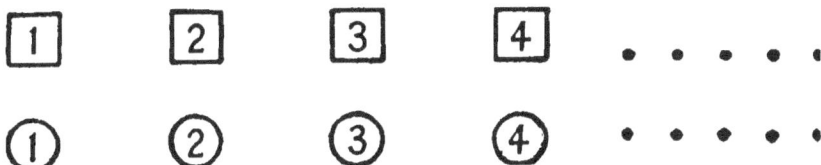

MUSIC.		MOVEMENTS.
		(Duple minor-set.)
A	1—4	First man turns second woman.
	5—8	Second man turns first woman.
B1	1—4	First and second men take hands, move forward between first and second women and cast off to places, first man to his left, second man to his right.
	5—8	First and second men turn once-and-a-half round and change places; while first and second women do the same (progressive).
B2	1—4	Women do as men did in B1.
	5—8	Partners turn.

JUICE OF BARLEY.

Longways for as many as will; in one part
(8th Ed. 1690).

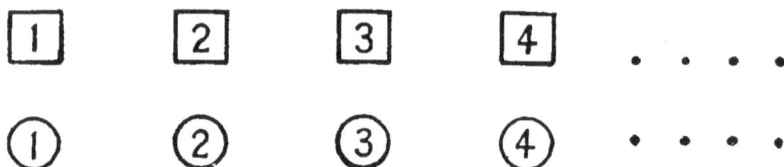

| 1 | 2 | 3 | 4 | . . . . |
| (1) | (2) | (3) | (4) | . . . . |

MUSIC.		MOVEMENTS.
		(Duple minor-set.)
A	1—4	First man and first woman go back-to-back; while second man and second woman do the same.
	5—8	Partners turn.
B1	1—4	First man, followed by second man, passes between first and second woman, turns to his right into second place, second man turning to his left into first place.
	5—8	All clap hands on the first beat of the fifth bar and go hands-four once round.
B2	1—4	First woman, followed by second woman, passes between first and second men, turns to her left into second place, second woman turning to her right into first place (progressive).
	5—8	As in B1.

MAIDS' MORRIS.

Longways for as many as will; in one part
(8th Ed. 1690).

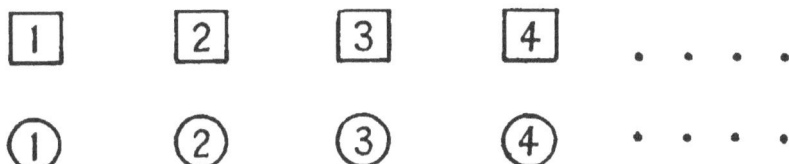

| 1 | 2 | 3 | 4 | . . . . |
| (1) | (2) | (3) | (4) | . . . . |

MUSIC.		MOVEMENTS.
		(Duple minor-set.)
A	1—4	First and second men take hands, fall back a double, and then move forward a double to places, turning single as they do so.
	5—8	First and second women do the same.
B1	1—2	First and second couples hands-four four slips clockwise.
	3—4	All four turn single.
	5—6	First and second couples hands-four four slips counter-clockwise to places.
	7—8	All turn single.
B2	1—6	Circular-hey to places, four changes, partners facing.
		First man leads first woman down the middle into second place; while second man and second woman cast up into the first place (progressive).

LILLI BURLERO.

Longways for as many as will ; in one part (8th Ed. 1690).

| 1 | | 2 | | 3 | | 4 | | • | • | • | • |

| ① | ② | ③ | ④ | • | • | • | • |

MUSIC.		MOVEMENTS.

(Duple minor-set.)

A   1—4   First man and first woman lead down the middle below second couple, cast up and return to places.

5—8   Second man and second woman lead up the middle, cast down and return to places.

B1   1—2   First man and second woman change places.

3—4   First woman and second man change places.

5—6   All fall back a double.

7—8   All move forward a double, turning single as they do so.

B2   1—2   First and second men cross over and change places with their partners.

3—4   First and second men move backward each into the other's place : while first and second women do the same.

5—8   Circular-hey, three changes, partners facing (progressive).

POOL'S HOLE.

Longways for as many as will; in one part (8th Ed. 1690).

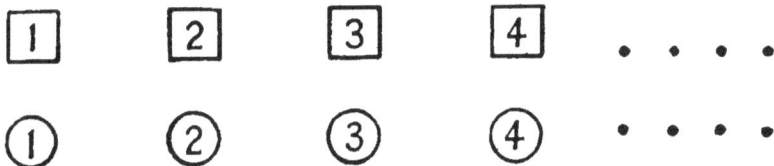

MUSIC.		MOVEMENTS.
		(Duple minor-set.)
A	1—4	First man and first woman cast down into the second place, second couple moving up into the first place. First woman then passes counter-clockwise round second man into the second place on the men's side; while first man passes clockwise round second woman into the second place on the women's side.
	5—6	First and second men change places.
	7—8	First and second women change places.
B	1—4	First and second couples hands-four.
	5—8	First and second couples progressive-hey, three changes, first man and first woman beginning the movement by passing by the right (progressive).

KING OF POLAND.

Longways for as many as will; in one part
(10th Ed. 1698).

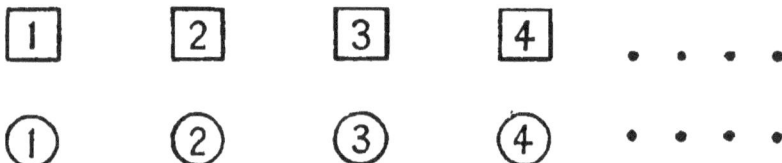

1	2	3	4	• • • •
①	②	③	④	• • • •

MUSIC.		MOVEMENTS.
		(Duple minor-set.)
		Throughout this dance the leading couples are improper. Partners on reaching the top or bottom of the Set must therefore remember to change places.
A	1—4	The first couple being improper, first man and second woman turn once-and-a-half round and change places; while second man and first woman do the same.
	5—8	First and second men cross over and change places with their partners, and then, turning their partners half-way round, fall back to the same places.
B1	1—2	First couple leads up to the top; while second man and second woman cast down into the second place.
	3—6	Circular-hey, three changes, partners facing (progressive; improper).
B2	1—6	First woman and first man cross between second man and second woman and pass, the first woman clockwise round second woman, the first man counter-clockwise round second man, meet, turn half-way round and fall back to places.